CREATING OUR PATHS TO WHOLENESS

ARVIND UPADHYAY

The significant problems we face cannot be solved at the same level of thinking we were at when we created them. — Albert Einstein

Creating Our Paths to Wholeness is the image of the quartered circle. Ancient quartered circles like the Celtic Eightfold Year Cycle and the Native American Medicine Wheel, along with their modern versions are found on many continents, at the center of many cultures. Wherever they have emerged, quartered circles have symbolized the inclusion of all reality within a cycle of wholeness. Just as the modern western world conceives of itself within a particular physical universe theorized by Sir Isaac Newton, ancient and indigenous civilizations understood their existence in relation to their conceptions of the forces of the universe. They understood the quartered circle as representing a cycle of change charged by the solstices and equinoxes, and the interrelatedness of other dualisms. The four seasons, the four directions, and corresponding myths about deities and humankind were associated with the thresholds of the quartered circle. Rites of passage and other rituals reenacted the shared myths. The fundamental difference between ancient or indigenous and modern scientific worldviews of reality is that we see the physical as split off from the spiritual. The ancient quartered circle represents the crossing of the horizontal axis of the temporal world and the vertical axis of the transcendent. Although in the post–Newtonian Western world we have learned to accept that science is based upon proof and beliefs are based upon faith, in effect the authority of the scientific has become a belief system or modern myth. Humans cannot help but make meaning. We conserve our truths in cultural artifacts like myths and enact them in our daily rituals. The ancients told myths of supernatural forces to make meaning of their existence; in the Western world we tell scientific myths. People may believe in other explanatory systems, but the essential myth of the modern Western world since the Enlightenment derives from Newtonian physics and the scientific method. We rely on empirical evidence. The laboratory with its measuring devices is used to isolate empirical truths. We learn this means of truth seeking in elementary school. Under the controlled conditions of a lab experiment, the same results can be reproduced. Every action has an equal and opposite reaction. Causes produce predictable effects. But not all experiences can be verified in the lab. Our lives, our organizations, and even natural phenomena like the weather, show patterns that cannot be replicated under the controlled conditions of a lab, or those of a therapy office. Yet there is predictability to these unpredictable systems. The new sciences are addressing these challenges to the Western scientific myth by looking at whole systems rather than at their parts. Chaos theory, like ancient traditions contemporary with the first quartered circles, proposes that all reality as we know it is only the explicate manifestation of a holomovement or an implicate universe. The nature of this implicate whole is illustrated by the Heizenberg's uncertainty principle, the wave/particle theory of quantum physics. According to this theory the physical universe is made of waves and particles. When we are looking at particles we cannot look at the waves; when we are looking at waves, we cannot look at particles. Taken together, these complementary opposites that contradict each other empirically, constitute a whole larger than the sum of its parts. Wave and particle are complimentary aspects of the explicate world that together manifest an implicate reality. Newtonian physics can reproduce waves or particles in the lab, but not the complimentary aspect of both, or the implicate whole.

Contents

Foreword

A story is like water that you heat for your bath. It takes messages between the fire and your skin. It lets them meet, and it cleans you! Very few can sit down in the middle of the fire itself like a salamander or Abraham. We need intermediaries. A feeling of fullness comes, but usually it takes some bread to bring it. The body itself is a screen to shield and partially reveal the light that's blazing inside your presence. Water, stories, the body, all the things we do, are mediums that hide and show what's hidden. Study them, and enjoy this being washed with a secret we sometimes know, and then not. —Rumi

1
The Healing Circle

The equal–ended cross, surrounded by a circle, a pattern found in many countries, is taken as the oldest symbol of consciousness, of integration. Our consciousness splits life into qualities, and so we know the tension of opposites, the basic differentiation. But the opposites are also the cross and you; if steadfast enough we may feel the stillness at the centre, and if acceptance is possible, our own arms encircle us and we contain our pain. The Healing Circle is a pattern of self organization that came to me in a shamanic journey three years before I used it as an organizing metaphor for a presentation. Returning to ordinary reality from the journey state, I was so impacted that I drew the image in a notebook. I was not yet conscious of its full significance to my work. The complexities of emergent self organization would have to wait another ten years to become part of the whole meaning of the image. It awaited emergence at the edge between the order and chaos of my life.

In the absence of a unifying cultural mythology, we live personal mythologies. Unlike a linear model of development or a particular myth (such as Freud's use of the Oedipal myth), a personal mythology is a collection of interconnected stories. Most of these stories we have consciously adopted or crafted to explain our experiences of living to ourselves or to explain ourselves to others. However, the most important stories are usually unconscious. They are stories that have self organized outside of our conscious awareness around a few central themes that bring meaning and purpose to our lives. These stories operate invisibly and generate the recurring patterns of our successes and failures in living. Our personal myths determine our individual experience of reality. When our internal and external realities are largely congruent, they operate optimally.

We can become aware of our personal myths when external reality impinges upon our internal reality, when they no longer work to organize reality for us, or when they are incongruent. Out of such chaos new order can emerge. Our lives seem to be linear as time and language seem to be linear. But it is easy enough to recount experiences of life and time that cannot be forced into linearity. Our lives are like poetry, in which the repetitions and patterns of language deepen the meaning of the linear sentence. The courses of our lives are cyclical. Even biologically, we repeat ourselves. We recycle the stages of our early development as we go through subsequent beginnings, connections, challenges, and reconstructions. As a template rather than a prescriptive, linear model for human development, the Healing Circle allows us to observe our apparently linear lives as a recycling of our personal mythologies at many levels. By seeing the recurrence of our personal myths around a cycle instead of as some pathology or repetition compulsion, we can begin to investigate how they have organized the range of behaviors or possibilities for living available to the self. The Healing Circle is a template which locates the transitions from one phase of development to the next, indicating where, according to our personal mythologies, we are likely to get stuck because we are without the skills or emotional experiences to make these transitions. As an ancient symbol of the whole of reality, the Healing Circle also represents personal mythologies in relation to other life cycles?those of other persons, other cultures, other life forms, and the whole of a physical and spiritual universe. It thus represents individual life as a microcosm of the whole of reality and its unfolding possibilities for interconnectedness with the whole of life. This perspective is in itself healing. It releases us from linearity and time and recovers what we cannot see: joy when we feel grief, anger when we feel powerlessness, our connectedness to others when we feel isolated. The Healing Circle can direct consciousness to an awareness of a fuller life.

The Western world has separated itself from the cycles of nature philosophically and technologically. The use of the quartered circle may offer healing in part because it is a return to a relationship with nature akin to those of indigenous cultures. But even for those of us living in the "modern world" the seasons have not lost their affective power nor have we lost our relationship to the cycle they repeat. We may be able to have air?conditioning in summer or central heating in winter, controlling the effects of the seasons, but we have not, as yet, lost our connection with them. They continue to move us. They surround us through cultural artifacts, symbols, memories, and, of course, stories. While the characteristics of the seasons vary from latitude to latitude, the cycle of the seasons and its repetitions within us are still deeply familiar and perhaps even more affecting for us in the modern world when we find ourselves in harmony with them despite our ways of forgetting them. The Healing Circle might first be understood as a template. As an ancient model it is usually referenced to the cycle of seasons. The alchemists of the middle ages saw it as a representation of the self. The seasons are still a familiar metaphor for the recyclings in our lives. Just as the earth undergoes a continuous recycling of the seasons, from the beginnings of spring, through the summer harvest, the challenge of the cooler, shorter days of fall into the cold incubation of winter back to spring's rebirth, so also do our ives and our lives' endeavors continuously recycle, with variations, round upon round, offering both the hope of change and the security of repetition.

Spring, the new beginning, is the protective holding environment. Summer, the ripening, is the meaningful connection with significant other(s). Fall, the preparation for winter, is the gradual challenge toward mastery, requiring a separation from the dependency on significant other(s); and Winter, the incubation, is the time for internalizing new structures, theorizing, and building updated models of reality. Human development over the life span can be seen through the template of the healing circle. Early stages of our development are largely time driven, pushing us forward stage by stage whether we complete them or not. To grow a self, the newborn human's developmental template requires a springlike protective holding environment, a meaningful harvest of connections to significant other(s), a gradual challenging towards mastery within a specific setting, and a fluid modeling of reality. If these requirements are not optimally met, the newly emerging self makes adjustments to get enough of what is missing or just to survive. These adaptations influence how development unfolds. These adaptations, then, affect the Healing Circle template, influencing all future recycling of developmental sequences. Unresolved developmental issues are reactivated as we recycle around the template or as we reencounter a situation requiring under developed skills. A developmental glitch in the Spring quadrant, for example, would be activated each time we cycled through Spring or each time we began some thing new, like a dependency on someone. Evolution has thus created a failsafe mechanism assuring that we might discover our eventual wholeness.

In the Healing Circle pattern, the solstices and equinoxes generate the four general kinds of rituals. These celestial events are significant markers in myth and ritual through the ages and cultures of human beings. Monuments have been built to measure and commemorate them. Stonehenge in England seems to have been built to use the summer solstice, as was the Great Medicine Wheel in Wyoming. Both these structures are quartered circles. While the specific purposes of Stonehenge are lost, we can imagine that the Great Medicine Wheel was part of the Plains Indians' ceremonials involving the Sun Dance, a profound celebration of thanksgiving, growth, prayer, sacrifice, and cultural renewal still conducted today during the time of the summer solstice. Easter, a vernal equinox celebration, and Christmas, a winter solstice celebration, are familiar examples. Indigenous cultures organize their rituals around the cycles of nature. Typically, colonizing cultures made use of these calendars referenced to the seasons, substituting their own rituals and holy days. I believe our connection with the cycles of nature and the rituals around them are projections onto nature of our human desire to know the whole of reality and to be participants in it. Thus the cycle of the seasons maps our own; repeatedly we make it our story. The Eight Gates: A Cycle of Change Many traditions have used the segmented circle to hold the complexity of living. Among some Native American tribes, the Spider, who with her eight legs is the weaver of all the infinite possibilities of creation, renders the web of life. Her legs represent the eight gateways of spirit—the four winds of change and the four directions. Many of you are familiar with the horoscope of astrology, another segmented circle. While it divides the circle into twelve segments and circles around counter–clockwise, it still represents a rich reservoir for complexity. In Tao of Chaos, Katya Walter (1998) demonstrates that the I Ching is essentially a complex dynamic system utilizing the same universal order of complementary chaos that DNA uses. The eight gates are represented by the eight trigrams of the "Old Family Mandala" of the I Ching (later expended to sixty–four hexagrams). In keeping with my own roots, I will extrapolate the eight gates of growth by using the Celtic Eightfold Year (King, 1994; Murray, 1988). Some things fit the quadrants by way of their association to the seasons; others belong to one quadrant or another because of their contextual relationships with each other. The same can be said for the elements assigned to the four boundary areas. Each of these eight phases of living has a "gateway" to it. Taken as parts to a whole, each gate marks both a passage of space through time and an entry into the implicate order or spirit world. I want to give you a flavor of each of the eight gates through a synthesis of a variety of mythic materials referenced to the four quadrants and the four dividing and quartering threshold crossings where rituals can organize changes. The Celtic eightfold year of the eight gates is a metaphor. In lived lives, we may be going through multiple processes simultaneously, like beginning a new relationship, making a job change, incubating a short story, and being elevated to the presidency of our professional organization, all in the same month of July. The quali- ties clustered in the gateways around the calendar are touchstones rather than absolutes. Gate 1: Keeping Still On the calendar, this gate occurs on February 2, and was called Imbolc by the Celts, Candlemas or St. Brigid's Day by the Christians and Ground Hog Day by others. This day celebrated motherhood and childbirth and the flow of milk. In the most dreary and depressing of our winters, the unlimited potentials for rebirth are incubating in virgin purity like crystals in stone. Pregnant virginity symbolizes the eternal fire that purifies the self making ready for the rebirth to come with the Spring. The fires have not died; an ember of the new beginnings is discovered. The imagery and symbolism of this gate are the wombs of growth: the labyrinth, the cave, the automobile, the Medicine Wheel, the pathless forest, the classroom—all wombs with views—in dreams and personal mythology. In its dark aspect there can be wombs without views—prisons, dungeons, deserts, coffins, and the countless cul de sacs and eddies in the stream of the life cycle. In every process, from living a life to learning something new, like tying a shoe, there is a time needed for rest and renewal, during which new behaviors experienced will be catalogued, assessed, and evaluated for future use in our behavioral repertoire. Most of this takes place out of conscious awareness, but we need time in isolation away from external stimuli to do it. In the cycle of the seasons, this is the Winter quadrant, from winter solstice to the vernal equinox. This is the dead of winter, where we surrender to the cold, the dark, the seasonal slowdown of activity, and our own need for introspective self evaluation. Time hangs heavy upon us, like snow on the rooftops; where incubating our new potentials, like seeds in the ground, often feels more like laying fallow in the frozen mud; and when we can get cabin fever waiting for spring. This is the Great Mysterious, indeed. Philosophically, we are experiencing the mystical view of life, wherein all things are interconnected. The archetypes occurring in myths emerging from this gate include the Hermit, the Teacher or Great Master, the Fool, the Prince or Princess (especially on the return run from a major test), and the Virgin (sometimes pregnant) Goddess (like the Virgin Mary or Saint Brigid). Thematically, these are the stories of Paradise Regained, when a compassionate Self empathetically under-stands the connectedness of all things, a Self so expansive it can role reverse with the Universe or any part of it. Throughout the so–called Dark Ages, the Alchemists spent a lot of time, when they were not trying to make gold out of the four elements, seeking the mythical philosopher's stone—the touch of which had magical healing powers. In this so–called Modern Age, we seek such magic in ideas and knowledge. And to tell the truth, there is a kind of philosopher's stone in the power of an idea and/or ritual procedure. Such structures can transform emotion, change behavior, expand wants, or reframe a conceptual universe. These kinds of structures are the essence of the Winter quadrant and they have tremendous power to hinder or heal. Much of therapy is discovering the hindering structures and prescribing or developing the healing ones. Gate 2: The Clinging On the calendar, this gate comes in late March. It is the Spring Equinox, the day when the hours of light and darkness are equal. This gate celebrates the return of the sun by exploring the theme of rebirth and renewal in the groups we belong to, the family system, or our communities, large and small. The family, however, is the first soil our self–seeds encounter. This is a time when the personal myths that inhibit or enhance the possibilities of our emergence become manifest. For one reason or another, we decide that we are too bad, wrong, sinful, worthless, stupid, inconsiderate, macho, feminine, or what have you, to be accepted—or not. Special attention is directed to the ways we purify ourselves in order to become incorporated into the communities to which we belong. This is a time of ritual cleansing of the inevitable accumulation of unexpressed feelings, misunderstandings, secrets, and hurts, intended and unintended, that human beings seem heir to. It returns us to a state of relative innocence regardful of our age and experience. Moreover, after a winter's worth of incubating and integrating, the new and changed version of oneself is ready to emerge into new adventures, ready for anything, including self acceptance. If one is not ready for this, rites of incorporation are at hand to help. These are rituals, like Lent, that purify the self of con- flicting beliefs and behaviors and that clear the way to a birthing of a new belonging. Sometimes, the traumatic events that place us in this quadrant are thrust upon us. A formerly Catholic client comes for help for sexual impotence. Everything had been fine until he and his wife decided it was time for a baby. This story unfolds: As a teenager, he impregnated his girl friend. They secretly had the baby aborted at a clinic, separated, and went on with their lives. Although he felt some guilt, he believed that they had done the right thing. Later work uncovers deep loss and unexpressed grief over the death of a beloved grandfather when he was five and considered too young to attend funeral services. The loss of the baby had activated this unexpressed grief and he began to work this through. Eventually, the following curative ritual for the last baby is designed. He is to find a symbolic object to represent his aborted child, who he felt was a son. He is to carry this object with him at all times for six weeks (the length of time the fetus lived), during which time he is to abstain from sexual activity. He is, on the other hand, to talk to this object (his son) daily. At the end of the six weeks, he is to create a funeral ceremony for his son. Three days later, he is to resume sexual activity. We have many purification rituals: Sweat lodges and showers, grueling physical workouts, mikvahs and brises, baptisms and penances, amends and atonements of all kinds. Much of therapy is the cleansing of unnecessary garbage and the incorporation of information so that new energy can be claimed for life. Some movies that illustrate this passage are The Abyss, Aliens, How to Make an American Quilt, and Nell. Gate 3: The Joyous On the calendar, this is May 1. The Celts called it Beltane, and it was a fertility celebration. Thematically, it is concerned with new beginnings. First days at school, first best friends, first fights, first failures, first dates, and the first inklings of our life's purpose. This is the time to determine to what degree and quality these first experiences have effected our other beginnings in life. In the cycle of the seasons, this is the Spring quadrant. All images of new beginnings point to this gate. Images of Paradise, the Golden Age, Abundance, Perfection, and the Gift (receiving what your heart desires) abound. It is about love, support, and nurturance. It is the time of the Mother (and Child), the Nurse, the Caretaker, and the Demi–Gods or –Goddesses. Nurturance is not just being nice. It is a complex set of behaviors (feelings, wants, actions, and beliefs) that require knowledge of the recipient, a sense of timing and appropriateness, and a matching of stroke, stroker, and strokee. Nurturance nourishes the growth of new babies and new beginnings. It involves a sense of what's enough on the part of the giver and the receiver, and the receiver must have done the necessary incorporations and purifications to believe in deserving the nurturance given. This is also about becoming a King or Queen of the May. You have integrated some important life experiences by incubating them for a period of creative isolation. And you have accepted the consequences. And you have also found significant others to affirm them in you. What happens next? You get to be a star! You get to express yourself the best you can and the people around you take delight in and nurture that self expression. This is the attraction of the star position. However, people who are not stars will want to get close to you for a little of your sparkle. People want you to keep expressing yourself as you have been without changing or they want you to grant them their wishes. Somehow the piper has to pay, and the warm milk and honey showered upon you starts flowing the other way. You are nurturing them! Your achievements become an obligation for continued performances. And everybody wants to bask in the shine of your sparkle. And you feel all alone and, yes, isolated (again). That is the repulsion of the star position. Among the pre-Roman Celts, kingship was a terminal disease. A king might be ritually sacrificed for the future of the clan (Frazer, 1961). This gate explores the natural history of the positive star position and some of the attractions and repulsions of that role. In the cycle of selfness, we all need to pass through the star position to fuel up for the rest of the journey of the eternal return around the Healing Circle. We all need to be King or Queen—for a day. On the calendar, this gate is the Summer Solstice. It happens in late June and is the celebration of the longest day of the year. Balance is the theme of this gate: Balance, continuity, the breath of life, and the half heard, half felt call to adventure that lures us onward and out of balance again. Investiture to King or Queenship, our elevation to the peak, is the back-story of a reawakening to the nature of wanting, the experience of joy (transcendent connectedness), the pain of disappointment, and the essence of the spiritual. The mystery of why we begin to feel trapped by the very things we yearned for is embedded in the cycle of the seasons: after the solstice, only one day of glory, the days begin to shorten, the long night begins to return. And our wants have turned into have–tos. And the people who have thought that we were great feel very demanding in their admiration. Well, to hell with them, we might want to say. Unfortunately, before we can let go of that to which we are holding fast, we must accept, acknowledge, and understand all that we have and are and our investment in it. We learn very early in life that glory at the top is not that easy to let go of, no matter how trapped we feel. This gate, therefore, focuses on the rites of continuity that help us own our investment in ourselves and our things and separate the two so that we can move on. The rites of continuity within our own community also set our place in the community so that we may connect with others and cooperate productively in the affairs of the group. Rites of continuity bring about Apotheosis, which is a term that describes what happens when Clark Kent slips into the phone booth and exits as Superman. Apotheosis means exaltation to divine rank or status. In the human context, it means rising to and claiming publicly the growth and values of our stages of development throughout our life cycles. Rites of continuity include receiving awards, crowns, medals, and degrees. Family dinners, potlucks, and potlatches can be rites of continuity. The production and presentation of art to a community or the implementation of new skills and personal myths acquired through the hard work of personal growth are also rites of continuity. Contact, It's a Wonderful Life, Resurrection, and Secrets and Lies are movies that tell stories of rites of continuity.

Gate 5: The Gentle On the calendar, this gate comes in late July or early August. The Celts called it Lughnasa. This is the harvest time, and a time for mourning. Yet the focus is on peak experiences, those fruits of living that make life joyous. This gate explores personal peak experiences and ways of sharing them within our communities. On the circle of the seasons, this is the Summer quadrant. This was also the time of the Celtic games, chariot races and swordplay, and the time when trial marriages for a year and a day could be declared. With the discovery of agriculture, human beings could count on a steady and frequently surplus food supply to harvest. With locally dependable abundance, we shattered the mirror of the hunter?gatherer lifestyle that the environment presented to show us who we were and what we were on this earth to do. Since that time, we have been creating models to mirror ourselves, and each model that we have created shatters as our experience of reality changes, giving birth to new aspects of our human nature. From the Cosmic to the Family levels, mirrors are shattered and pasted back together again in a myriad of ways. Through this gate, we encounter Paradise Lost. This is the time of the Trickster, the Clown, the Betrayer, and the Dark Double, Mr. or Mrs. Hyde. It is the time for the call to adventure, where the perceived incongruities of our existence spur us on to seek redemption. One of the biggest tricks in life is the illusion of the endless summer. Where there is summer can fall be far behind? This gate is about breaking out of the illusions of life in order to expand our awareness to view our lifepath as less stable but richer with possibilities. And the gods come, invoked or not. These new possibilities intrude upon our awareness whether we like it or not. These calls to the adventure of new growth can be hard or soft, but we perceive them as betrayals, and we look for culprits to blame. Gate 6: The Abysmal This gate is the Autumnal Equinox. It comes in late September. It deals with rites of separation that initiate us into the mysteries of true maturity. Just as the sun with-draws, making way for winter, our Mothers (and all of our alma Maters) withdraw from us (or we from them). We struggle with feelings of betrayal, fear of failure, and behavioral paralysis, and we resist the thrust towards our own identity and the death of our dependence. We must negotiate our way towards our personal quest for identity. Rites of separation include being stripped of our clothes, belongings, gender, and/or status, being made carriers of our community hope, and/or being placed in seclusion. In primitive cultures, these rites of passage were what marked a youngster's passage into full community membership as an adult. They often involved mutilation of some kind (circumcision, scarification, tattooing, hair cutting, bloodletting) to mark an external change on the body to correspond to the inner change in the psyche. They involve loss and letting go of the old, and the instruction of the initiate in new information, new ways of thinking, and new skills. All members of the community are expected to be initiated and to pass this test successfully. In modern culture, we have few if any rites of passage. The ones we do have are neither universal nor always passable. Driver licensing, sporting tests, military service, or graduation from school are not enough to balance the losses. Naturally, we therefore resist losing and letting go. The kite that flies is the kite that offers resistance to the wind. Similarly, the person that grows best is the one who offers resistance to the pressures for change. This resistance is the doorway to unresolved issues from childhood, unexpressed feelings in the present, illnesses, accidents, blame frames, numb outs, and you name its. The pressure to change comes both from ourselves and from others in our lives who want us to work harder, express more feelings, love better, work less, be cleaner, smarter, or whatever. All of this makes great sense and value from their point of view—and some of it makes sense from our point of view. The energy between what's right for them (the wind), and what seems right to us (the kite) runs down the string to the Self that Holds Everything: The Kite is Flying! Sometimes it's great fun; then again, at other times, lightning strikes. The outcome is greater self knowledge and identity, because we learn what we want and need for ourselves. Then we can do or learn to do what we must to get what we want and need. This gateway explores the joys and pains of resisting the pressure put on us by the world, our friends and family, and our own inner parts. The more we resist, the longer the process, but the greater the reward. Rites of separation help us transform our identities and claim new roles in our communities. Some movies that illustrate rites of separation are Fly Away Home, Into the West, King of the Hill, National Velvet, and The Wizard of OZ. Gate 7: The Arousing On the calendar, this gate occurs on November 1, the festival of the dead. The Celts called it Samhain, the Christians, All Saints' Day, and today secular folk focus on the day before, Halloween. This is the Fall quadrant. In Celtic times this could be the time that one was called upon to endure pain or death courageously in order to maintain the kingdom. An important archetype is the Hero's journey into the underworld (the unconscious), his or her near–death ordeal, and the return to the light of day with new resources. This gate conveys images of death, pain, and courage: Abduction, Dreams, a Journey to the Underworld, a Night– Sea Journey (maybe in a Whale's Belly), Brother/Sister Battle, Dismemberment, Crucifixion, and the Sacrificial Death. It involves the slaying of dragons on a road of physical trials and tests of wit. One encounters witches, trolls, ogres, the Antagonist, and many magical and unexpected helpers. Within the context of the cultural mythology, the stories of Persophone and her mother, Demeter, Gilgamesh and his beloved Enkidu, Jesus and his apostles, and Ripley and Newt (from the movie Aliens) are relevant. Individually, we all have dark passages in our lives just as important to our personal mythologies as these cultural myths are to the cultures that birthed them. This gateway deals with the experience of rejection and with how rejection, as part of the cycle of ongoing personal development, invites personal growth. We also experience "stuckness," where the movement in the cycle has eddied and flowed back upon itself, when the fear of rejection causes us to stall our journey. At the same time, it is a doorway to positive personal change and self transformation. One of the by–products of all the tests and struggles is the development of new skills and competencies. We eventually become what we have done. These are the stories of the Quest for Redemption.

Gate 8: The Receptive On the calendar, this is the Winter Solstice. It comes in late December. The Celts called it Yule, the Romans, Saturnalia, and the Christians, Christmas. One of the results of winter is to keep people at home around the fire telling the stories that carry the meaning and purpose of life and the rules and roles of living in their particular culture. Interpersonal relationships are often sorted out in this time of restoration as well. The Winter Solstice, the ultimate story night, is the shortest day and the longest night of the year. As the beginning of the return of the sun, it is also the threshold of transformation, after which the seasons will unfold in their familiar form but with renewed content. It is time to come in out of the cold, winterproof our living spaces, and prepare for changes of an inner sort. This is a time of core changes. To prompt these changes, we engage in rites of transformation. A rite of transformation is a ritual of healing that assists the celebrant in changing some condition that prevents attainment of a desired state of being. It brings about the death of the ego and the rebirth of the self. The changes take place in the beliefs, the personal mythology, of the celebrant. At some point when you are out there all by yourself (rejected by one and all, including yourself, and totally helpless to do anything about it) you surrender. You stop all the fussing and put your trust in some other power to move on. Miracles occur when choices are reduced to one, the unknown possibilities. You are completely free; with nothing left to lose, you have everything to gain. Rites of transformation generally involve four basic themes. One is resolving the feelings of betrayal and guilt through Father (or Mother) Atonement. Two is uniting our inner male and female in a Sacred Marriage. Three is the theft of a myth changing lesson from the jaws of death in the underworld through Mother (or Community) Atonement. Four is the elevation of the hero or heroine to a new state of being through Apotheosis after the death of his or her ego– bound fears and desires. These rituals help us to change at a deep, cellular level of knowledge (gnosis). Thus they require an intensification that can be called a blood sacrifice. This does not mean that we shed actual blood but that we surrender some ego grasping understanding of others, the world, or ourselves, grieve its death, and embrace the reborn shivering self. Evidence suggests (Grof, 1988) that in order to cross thresholds into altered states of knowing, barriers need to be passed, from the cultural conserve of the existing personal mythology to the spontaneously experienced, uncharted possibilities, usually through stimulation (not too much, not too little). These are the opportunities to close the gap between our ideal and our actual self?images. This theme is regularly presented in literature and in films like Braveheart, Breaking the Waves, Cool Hand Luke, On the Waterfront, and The Shawshank Redemption.

The Healing Circle suggests that life follows a cycle rather than a linear or chronological calendar. We recycle our personal mythologies at many levels and in all the quadrants. The eight gates of the Celtic year locate these recyclings in the process of the cycle of seasons and within cultural cycles referenced to them. The metaphors of the new beginnings of spring, the fruitfulness of summer, the foot dragging decline of fall, and the life in death of winter can be applied independent of the actual time of year. The beginning of something marks its springtime. The Healing Circle shows us what the cycle can be and gives meaning to the process. The ways in which the Circle has been used offer a rich integrated cultural lore on which we can draw to intuit the relationships of parts to whole in our experience of life. But, in fact, the quartered circle is a blank template around which any issue can be explored. The relationships of the four quadrants and the four thresholds remain the same while the contents can be anything that can be factored into these relationships. To the degree that we can tune our consciousness to the dynamic flow of universal life we will participate optimally in the evolutionary thrust of the universe and in our own lives; what is above, after all, is what is below. The healing the circle points to is the reconnection of the parts of a whole. We will connect with the beings around us—the other men, women, children, as well as the minerals, the plants, the animals, and all things that exist. We will live more spontaneously and creatively balanced between the weight of stultifying stability and the pull of chaotic change. The Healing Circle is a tuning fork for consciousness. The power of the Healing Circle as a meta?pattern or instrument for attending to the patterns of life is manifold. Through the Healing Circle we can see complexly enough to observe some of the dynamic systems which make up a person. It is applicable in multiple settings. It recovers us to our physical and cultural relationships to the cycle of the seasons. As a symbol, the Healing Circle has for centuries affected the human mind and spirit across cultures and con sciousness. As a structure it divides and connects the apparent polarities that make up the whole of experience. While the Healing Circle differentiates phases of our life cycles and the points of ritual crossing, it also offers an image of wholeness, providing a perspective on the thresholds at which we may experience the possibilities of life. The word heal comes from the Middle English word helen, which means "to make whole" or "to care about." The delivery of wholeness is the gift of the Healing Circle. Mandalas are symbols of the unity of the self. They are an archetype of wholeness. Mandalas unite masculine angularity with feminine circularity. Angularity is separating. Circularity is bonding. Mandalas are symbols of wholeness. According to Carl Jung, mandalas appear in dreams in times of stress, indicating a need for unity and a new emergence of the Self. The quartered circle is the archetype of the self. Archetypes are empirically derived postulates contained in the collective unconscious of all human beings (Jung, 1969).

Archetypes act like instincts in their capacity to shape conscious contents by regulating, modifying, and motivating them through distinctly numinous, spiritual effects. They manifest themselves only through their ability to organize images and ideas unconsciously. Once established, the conscious mind continues to elaborate the gnosis of the symbol. Jung's studies suggested that a human mind is determined by complementarity, a subject coming in the next chapter. Consciousness complements unconsciousness and vice versa. They stand as opposites. The play between them and the functional balances achieved among their self similar properties determines the reality we experience unfolding. According to Jung, equivalent opposites are necessary conditions inherent in the act of cognition (Jung, 1978). Without them there is no cognition! The interplay and balance of opposites into functional union is a prerequisite for wholeness.

2

The Mystery of the Circle: Complementary Opposition

————◦♡◦————

You have noticed that everything an Indian does is in a circle, and that is because the Power of the world always works in circles, and everything tries to be round. Everything is done in a circle. The sky is round, and I have heard the earth is round like a ball, and so are the stars. The wind in its greatest power, whirls. Birds make their nests in circles, for theirs is the same religion as ours. The sun comes forth and goes down again in a circle. The moon does the same and both are round. Even the seasons form a great circle in their changing, and always come back to where they were. The life of a man is a circle from childhood to childhood, and so it is in everything where Power moves.

The fundamental form of process is cyclical movement, the alternation of success and decline, effort and repose, life and death which is the rhythm of process.

Human beings live in time and the timeless. The meanings that we make of our experiences encrypt the complementary aspects of existence, holding them in character, plot, and symbol. Our unique choices transform the wave functions of our possibilities into particulate existence. Complementarity "particularizes" our lives while preserving the wholeness to which we can return. The Healing Circle is a window to the fundamental reality. It is a window to wholeness. The quartered circle incorporates the arrow of time and the timelessness of the deeper complementarity of reality. It provides a structure for apprehending both systems holistically: the unfolding of systems in time and their underlying timeless complementaries that determine what explication actually unfolds from the implicate order. The quartered circle is both complex and simple. It is a picture or archetype of fields of probability, of acausal or-deredness. The four seasons are more than an apt metaphor for the process of human growth and living. We often think of experience in fours, but when this perspective is missing the making of a quartered circle can help us find the whole of which a given perspective is a part. As a model of the interconnectedness of the implicate reality, the seasons are a template around which four seasonal aspects of an issue or idea can be unfolded. The Healing Circle illuminates relationships. The seasons of living cluster the space and time variables of life. The vertical axis points to the summer (above) and winter (below) solstices, the points of greatest disequilibrium in the earth's cycle around the sun. The horizontal axis points to the spring (left) and fall (right) equinoxes, the points of greatest equilibrium in the earth's journey. These axes mark the thresholds of the four seasons. The thresholds thus created between the seasons call for ritual procedures honoring the seasonal changes in ourselves. These thresholds cluster energy and momentum variables that establish the vectors of interconnection among the seasonal quadrants.

When a child's upbringing provides good enough experiences in the four early stages or seasons of development, the consequences are an ability to care for the self and heal. The child who is sufficiently nurtured (held, rocked, comforted, fed) is receptive to the subsequent stage of intruding (peek-a-boo, saying no, setting limits). Later, parents (or therapists) provide challenging (age appropriate lessons to learn skills like walking and talking, learning to take care of oneself) and ultimately the structuring of reality (how to calm oneself in bed, the names of things, how to create meaning, how to reason and express feelings). This child will learn self?soothing, authenticity, and a capacity to be dependent, independent and interdependent. She or he will be prepared through successfully meeting parental (or therapeutic) challenges to work through things and maintain a stable sense of self worth. Where nurturing, intruding, challenging, and structuring are inadequate, instead, the child will experience lovelessness, joylessness, powerlessness, or mindlessness in the respective quadrants. Adequate parental or therapeutic input will facilitate the four functions of consciousness: feeling, wanting/intuition, doing/sensation, and thinking. The tools for dependency will be appropriately developed, ranging from a capacity to be dependent, to one for interdependency, to one for co? and counter? dependency, to one for independence. And as life events erupt, threatening the functions of any quadrant, the core elements of the healing process will be available: trust, contact, action and awareness. These examples not only make sense, they also demonstrate the kind of relations among the quadrants of the Healing Circle. These relationships can be Commutable, Orthogonal, Complementary, and Complete. Relationships that are commutable share qualities that can be observed at the same time. They are essentially the same though accidental attributes are different. Spring and summer are commutable in that there is more daylight than darkness, and vice versa for fall and winter, where there is more darkness than light. Similarly, Nurturing and Intruding are commutable. Distinct as they are, they share the qualities of an interpersonal closeness in which the child's needs are met without him or her having to do anything.

Complementary relationships express a dual focus on two things that appear to be opposites. These two things appear mutually exclusive and cannot be held in consciousness simultaneously. Yet together they constitute a whole. Spring and Fall are complementaries. So are Summer and Winter. Like the particles and waves of light, these foci cannot be simultaneously observed, yet the observation of one creates its "opposite." In quantum physics, the wave and particle aspects of light are complementary. While they cannot be observed at the same time, but they are aspects of the same quantum stuff. They also interact. In complementary "opposites," there is a kind of necessity or correspondence. Looking back at the seasons, given the tilted rotation of the earth around the sun, spring, the part of the orbit that brings the earth closer to the sun, presupposes fall, the time when the orbit takes the earth away from the sun. The unobservable complementary is said to be encrypted (enfolded) into the observable one. Because of the tilt of the earth's axis in its orbit around the sun, the seasons spin through an alternation of commutable and complementary relationships to create an ebb and flow of equilibrium and disequilibrium that underlies human development. Referring to sample charts 21-26, nurturing and challenging are complementaries. There is a necessary relationship or correspondence between the two apparent opposites. Whereas nurturing is characterized by trusting interpersonal closeness, challenging functions through interpersonal distance. Trust in another person is encrypted in the self?trust required to face a challenge. Inversely, the capacity to let go of the self, a capacity for receptivity and merging, which the infant learns from sufficient nurturing, has encrypted within it the challenge of action. Yet for a healthy person, being nurtured or giving nurturance is not experienced as a challenge; and being faced with a challenge or presenting a challenge is not experienced as nurturing, no matter how necessary or empowering the successful mastery might be. In fact, as the Healing Circle illustrates, the experience of a challenge as nurturing or nurturing as a challenge would be diagnostic of developmental trouble, of something gone awry. The Healing Circle shows these complementaries to be unified, parts of a whole, in the unfolding and interrelated process of holomovement. The word Orthogonal describes relations that collide and bounce off each other. Ortho– means straight and –gon means angle, and orthogonal refers to things at right angles to each other. They are essentially different, locally noninteractive, and cannot be observed at the same time. Spring and Summer have more daylight than darkness; Fall and Winter have less daylight than darkness. Because of the global holism of the Healing Circle, orthogonality frequently enlightens and surprises; it highlights hidden aspects of the related fields. Intruding (Summer) and challenging (Fall) are orthogonal: Intrusion is interactive, challenge is singular. Yet intrusions are challenging and challenges intrusive. Orthogonal relationships are created by the unexpected, by what we would term traumatic. Relationships among the seasons of life are complementary and commutable, providing they are contiguous. There can be shocks as we pass through the equinoxes and solstices, but usually we know when to expect them. After all, some of our oldest archeological sites appear to be devices to anticipate, predict, and venerate these times. The orthogonal transitions are symbolized by the day and night, light and dark, good and bad, conscious and unconscious experiences that can turn a time around one hundred and eighty degrees. On the Seasons Cycle this is generally represented by the two halves separated by the line between the equinoxes. Later, when we encounter the generation of personal mythology, we will see how orthogonal shock can effect our lives. And finally, relationships are considered complete where everything is included and nothing is excluded that is part of the system. All complementaries are decoded and commutables and orthogonals accounted for. Completeness implicates holism. The Healing Circle and quantum physics are both systems for apprehending completeness, the whole that would not be knowable from the point of view of complementarity, commutability, or orthogonality alone. Developmentally, Self and Other begin as commutables (symbiosis), differentiate into orthogonals during the separation/ individuation process, then reconnect interactively as complementaries through projective identification (a necessary process to help us truly know ourselves), and, finally, when we have internalized a structure for it all, we will have completeness (that is, wholeness). The simpler the system, the more it will commute, and thus stay the same. Our expectations are built on the perception of simple systems. The more simple the system, the more reliable are our expectations, and the more difficult it is for us to apprehend the underlying complementarity. Expectations pave the road to hell and constancy is an illusion: commutability is only a part of the whole. Many of our personal myths, our created stories, are commutables, observed to make sense of our lives. Nevertheless, for every observation there will be a repression of complementary observations. These complementaries are encrypted in our hopes and dreams, our cultural myths, our symptoms, both physical and psychical, and our projections, horrific, human, and divine. Orthogonals, the impossible, are the doorways to understanding. Sooner or later we maneuver ourselves face to face with the impossible. The impossible usually turns out to be that which we could not see before, being blinded to complementaries by what we knew already. When we run into an orthogonal, we plunge into phase transition: That which we knew we no longer have and that which we have bumped into is impossible! Plexing the Circle I call the factoring of aspects of an idea around the quartered circle a fourplex or an eightplex, depending on whether four or eight phases are identified. The stem plex is from the word plexus, which is from the Latin word plectere, "to braid." A plex is a complexly interconnected arrangement of parts. One can create a fourplex for the seasonal quadrants or the thresholds between them. An eightplex refers to a factoring that includes all eight spaces of the template. Like the Healing Circle itself, plexing a theme can be simple and/or complex. To plex a theme requires both reason and intuition—and a good working vocabulary that can sort out connotating interferences. The Healing Circle can plex any theme by indicating the whole of which it is a part. A theme can be assigned to a quadrant using the touchstones of the seasons. It will have associations with one more than another, though depending upon the context of the issue it might be assigned to an alternative quadrant. So, for example, as a new beginning in the human life cycle, "birth" could belong to the spring quadrant. But if birth is in the context of human development it would more likely be placed in the winter quadrant and the circle would be plexed differently.

The quantum physicist, Niels Bohr, once said, "the opposite of a correct statement is a false statement. But the opposite of a profound truth may well be another profound truth." In this statement, the second example, the opposite of a profound truth, might also be stated, "the complementary of a profound truth is another profound truth." "After spring comes the summer" is a correct statement. One season follows the other. The folk wisdom that "A gentle spring makes a turbulent fall" may be a profound one, because it is connecting the two complementary seasons in a way that completes a whole, both in terms of the laws of nature and the two metaphors. Once the first set of complementaries for a theme is established a four part sequence may establish itself. The seasons or the circle are archetypes that influence reason and intuition to see the wholeness of complex things. Of course, the second set must be tested for complementarity In general, activities of the first quadrant, Spring, have to do with new beginnings and undifferentiated oneness; of the second quadrant, Summer, with the harvest of the fruits of our labors and meaningful contact with others. The third quadrant, Fall, introduces multilevels of complexity: We must handle competently all manner of challenges and coming endings. We must make preparations for the descent into the little deaths of getting bored with what we have done, needing to move on and learn new things, having to let go of the old first, and otherwise dealing with processes of recession and preparing for winter. The fourth quadrant, Winter, has to deal with the structuring of pattern and metapattern and the laying fallow of our internal fields so that new possibilities can come into being. Next, the set of four can be adjusted according to the other two kinds of relationships that obtain in the quartered circle: commutables and orthogonals. Commutables are qualities of a system that can be observed at the same time. Commutables are not polarities. They are sequential, linked in a change process in which one part flows into the other. They are essentially the same even though accidental attributes are different. Spring and summer are commutables because they are the time when there is more daylight than darkness. In essence, commutability is linear change. The sequences spring to summer, and fall to winter are on–going commutable relationships.

Moving to an abstract theme, the seasons can be used as a metaphorical map. If the theme is How can Therapy Heal? one might begin with the relationship between therapist and client which research has shown is the most important aspect of therapy (Consumer Reports, 1995; Seligman, 1995). Since this is a meaningful relationship with an other it could be placed in the second quadrant, Summer. Its complementary is in the fourth quadrant, Winter. The process of this quadrant, as the repeated use of the Healing

Circle demonstrates, is using new information to remodel reality. We might label this quadrant self teaching or the incorporation of teachings.

The Ritual Cycle Around the Healing Circle

I have alluded frequently to rituals and ritual processes. There is a whole chapter ahead delving into them. However, this is a good place to plex ritual while the associations of the process of plexing are warmed up. Like a compass that organizes the surround by quartering the directions, the Healing Circle helps us find our way in the sea of possibilities. As we go through experience we have a partial view; we go in one "direction." The healing circle is a method for recovering the whole to which our partial experience—if only temporarily—blinds us. Whatever we are experiencing in winter, or figuratively speaking, as a "winter" in our lives, is part of a cycle. The recovery of this perspective can help us get back to seeing our lives as a whole and seeing that whole in synchrony with the larger whole of experience itself. Plexing a theme around the Healing Circle heightens awareness of the seasons of living. It teaches us that all experience has an inherent wholeness that we can know and that living is a nonlinear process. Losses, for example, make way for new beginnings. In time, our confidence in the complementarity of reality allows us to feel joy in spite of pain, as well as pain in joy. As Ecclesiastes asserts, he or she that seeketh wisdom, seeketh grief. We can perhaps be reassured that aging is not a betrayal by the creator, but an opportunity to cycle through the seasons of living to find satisfaction, wholeness, and wisdom. There is a season for everything, and each round of the cycle provides renewed opportunities to sort through the process towards fulfillment of being. Because the thresholds deal with orthogonality, plexing them is more difficult than plexing the seasons. Plexing is about the form, not the content; the structure, the field of energy, rather than the content within the field. In plexing, the content is important only insofar as it informs the field. The Healing Circle is an archetypal form. According to Carl Jung, it is the archetype of the self. When we plex the circle, we order the stuff of human lives and life within the dynamical systems of energy, tension, and relatedness with the form itself. Complementarity suggests that commutablity and orthogonality emerge spontaneously from these relationships in the circle. This means that the "meaning" or qualities of the vertical axis are unobservable and separate from the "meaning" or qualities of the horizontal axis. In short, they are not always obvious. Therefore, the axes must be related rationally (which includes logic and feeling) to the context of the overall theme of the moment and particularly to the ritual cycle as well as the complete cycle of seasons and thresholds. Truth is not guaranteed and must be tested by experience. The four threshold crossings from one seasonal life process to another are symbolized by the moments when the earth is momentarily "still" in her circuit around the sun. These still points are the winter and summer solstices (solstice means "sun standing still") and the spring and fall equinoxes. While the relational dynamics that charge the daylight seasons (Spring and Summer) and the dark seasons (Fall and Winter) are between complementarity and commutability, the relational dynamics that charge the threshold between the daylight and darkness halves of the circle is between complementarity and orthogonality. The passage between them is dark and difficult; they correlate to the conscious self and the unconscious self.

The Healing Circle is like a shield between the self and the implicate chaos of possibilities, a shield taken down from our hearts and looked at as if seen in a mirror. Perhaps the first spiritual polarity that humankind projected onto the environment is that of the sky above, frequently perceived as male and the home of the ancestral grandfather, and the earth below, usually female and home of the grandmother or mother earth goddess. The person standing between, linking them in the present moment, had, looking out to the horizon arms outstretched, a right hand and a left and a head touching sky and feet touching earth. I like to think of the lone human being, standing on a hilltop, as the first felt orthogonal cycle. Within many cultural traditions, ancient and modern, the solstices and equinoxes have been identified with four kinds of ritual. I will have a great deal to say about rituals in a later chapter. I will broach the subject now in order to describe further the threshold crossings that the orthogonal and commutable relationships of the Healing Circle represent. In general, rituals help us cross the thresholds between seasonal phases. Crossing over commutable boundaries like Spring to Summer or Fall to Winter is easier than crossing the orthogonal boundaries of Summer to Fall or Winter to Spring because the orthogonal crossings require a refocusing of energy and attention. Each kind of ritual has a time and place in life and on the circle. Sometimes the seasons are too broad a stroke to be helpful and a finer duration is more helpful, as below: Beginning with the Sunset, the "end result" of the movement of the sun from day to night is separation. The sun seems to "go away." In the larger cycle of the Earth around the sun, it is actually the Earth that "goes away" from the sun, creating longer and longer nights until the longest night of the winter solstice. Thus the autumnal equinox marks the Rites of Separation, also known as the rites of passage or initiation. In traditional rites of passage, the celebrants (initiates) are removed from everyday affairs and attachments, usually in groups of youngsters coming of age in the same year. They are then instructed in how to behave in new ways, including how to feel, want, act, and think. They usually undergo an ordeal that often involves pain and sometimes mutilation, which changes them physically. They then return to the community as new beings, usually adults. All must undergo them, none will fail.

The Healing Circle of Personal Mythology

The Healing Circle apprehends both developmental time and the "eternal" timelessness of myth by holding the four part reality. Early childhood development is the template for the personal mythology; personal myths are the stories of our development. Human development is also affected by the cultural myths that organize the culture we grow up in. Myths, personal or cultural, are stories of the development of consciousness. Challenges to the continuance or quality of our existence force us to make choices in our lives as the quantum participant observers we are. These choices profoundly effect the unfolding of our unique perception of reality. Possessing completely different consciousness, no two people experience the same reality. And no one escapes the responsibility for making meaning. Erwin Schrödinger devised the cat–in–the–box paradox (known as the EPR paradox) in 1935 to help understand the role of the conscious observer in creating reality. A cat is in a box that has a 50/50 chance of releasing a lethal poison. Until someone looks in the box all possibilities exist (a condition Schrödinger mordantly described as "smeared"); in effect the cat is alive and dead. Once someone opens the box, becoming an observer, the wave possibilities collapse, and a particle is released. The cat is either alive or dead. At that moment, the observer decides whether the cat is alive or dead and so does the cat! At a quantum level, the level of micro reality, observation determines reality, and we have no idea how a particle decides to be a whole wave or a particle. On a macro level, the one that we live on anyway, the cat's decision is important too. It is much easier believing the cat can make decisions. If the issue is a little boy and an annihilating father, it is more complex. The child decides to live; the father decides the boy is "dead," an object to be used. The boy creates a personal myth of this experience that allows him to function in the world, but in a limited way. His myth carries within its complementaries the seeds of his redemption. The father, too, has a mythology that limits his perception of the "aliveness" of his son. And the father, too, has the seeds of redemption encrypted in the complementarities of his personal mythology. But both decisions effect the unfolding of reality. Events in our lives push us to determine the nature of our reality. Yet every choice encrypts the unchosen possibilities. Thus, in the complementarity of life, we measure our identities and preserve our possibilities.

3

Dynamics of Change

These motions of life have direction. Life moves toward wholeness. It seeks coherence. This is a journey of paradox that pursues a clear direction. It is paradoxical because the path seems first to move away from wholeness to developing a self that is unique and alone. But even the creation of unique selves is an example of coherence. Every self makes sense. It creates a world and an identity that feels coherent to itself. From infinite possibilities, it chooses what to notice and how to respond. All living things create themselves by this sensemaking process of perception and response. . . . Life pursues a path of differentness to a destination of wholeness. . . . Life coheres into selves and systems. In its great cohering motions, life is a poet. It brings together seemingly separate elements to create and discover new meaning. Life moves, creating more of itself in the unlimited space of wholeness.

Chaos, Order, and Complexity

The cultural myths of Order emerging out of Chaos are at least as old as human history (Abraham, 1994). But the actuality is more awesome than mysterious. The new sciences describe a reality that "wants to" connect. Elementary particles "want to" come together into more complex structures. Electrons "want to" make their quantum leaps to new more optimal states of being. In cosmology, the expanding universe has evolved from a dense undifferentiated mass to myriad of complex galaxies. In biology, survival of the fittest is only half of the story. The other half is that organisms evolve to a state of optimal disorderliness called complexity, a state poised between stability and change, where new order emerges spontaneously (Kauffman, 1993). "Life seeks order in a disorderly way," summarize Wheatley and

Kellnor–Rogers (1996): "Life uses processes we find hard to tolerate and hard to believe in—mess upon mess until something workable emerges." This complexity is everywhere, so ubiquitous that we do not notice it any more than the air we breathe, if reasonably clean. Yet from mundane moments of choice making to sacred flashes of intuition, we have all experienced emergence of new order from seeming disorder. Nowhere does the need for cognitive reconstruction become more necessary than in the study of chaos theory and complex dynamical systems. Research (Cosmides, 1989) has shown that reasoning is context dependent. The subject matter we are asked to reason about seems to regulate how we reason. This is a consequence of "form defined" explicate reality. However, when we are asked to reason about a subject for which we have no or few categories of comparison, we are at a loss. Perhaps a poet is prepared to comprehend the reality of complexity theories; the rest of us are held more or less captive by linear thinking about reality and mechanistic science. "The mechanistic image of the world is a very deep image, planted at subterranean depths in most of us" (Wheatley and Kellnor–Rogers, 1996). Some of our deep perceptions are simply habits of seeing and experiencing that translate into behaviors and some are culturally embedded beliefs about the nature of the world. Both effect the reality we observe. From quantum physics, we know that the observer effects reality. As Margaret Wheatley and Myron Kellnor–Rogers put it, "every act of observation loses more information that it gains. Whatever we decide to notice blinds us to other possibilities. In directing our attention to certain things, we lose awareness of everything else. We collapse the world of possibilities into a narrow band of observation" (1996). Humberto Maturana and Francisco Varela (1992) note that what we observe around us is more influenced by who we have decided to be than what is objectively there. What the eye picks up from the outside, for example, only accounts for twenty percent of what we use to create perception. The other eighty percent is comprised of information already stored internally as a function of who we are. Thus "every change is fostered by a change in self-perception" (Wheatley and Kellnor–Rogers, 1996). This is why all meaningful change requires the development of conscious awareness, which is our tool to engage with the process of self organization. To change conscious awareness we have to break into that internal eighty percent. When I refer to chaos in this book, I am referring to the technical term, deterministic chaos, not the word used in everyday conversations to complain about disorganization, inefficiency, carelessness, and messy living rooms.

Deterministic chaos means the integral presence of randomness where the parameters of the system evolve according to probability rather than deterministic cause and effect (Çambell, 1993). This leads to uncertainty in making predictions. The chaos in the new science is neither evil nor randomly haphazard. The stuff of human existence does not fall around the Healing Circle in classical chaotic random; nor is it placed there merely because that is "the way it has always been done." The universal drive towards complexity and multiple options, human development, complementarity, uncertainty—these dynamics operating at the edge between chaos and order—direct the patterning of human lives. When I refer to chaos in this book, unless I indicate otherwise, I refer to the possibilities ebbing and flowing within the interlocking web of multi–causes and effects. It is as if there were, indeed, a first cause; there seems to be an intentionality within the implicate universe. It seeks energetic optimal organization. Optimization does not involve perfection, it involves the intrusion of the implicate into the explicate, and the transcendence of the explicate reality back into the realm of the implicate. I will demonstrate that the human psyche is a spontaneously self organizing dynamic system poised on the edge between chaos and order, capable of both infinite bursts of evolutionary change and constructed periods of frozen stability. Human consciousness is self referential, and is thus nonlinear. A person can be successful in childhood. Later when faced with a failure, that person can refer back to the earlier success. The outcome is unpredictable. The past success can be a resource or a rebuke, depending upon its relationship to other life experiences from the past or in the moment. Each self reference is an iteration of the past recycling into the present. The quartered circle is a representation of these recyclings. Before I demonstrate this, a little history about chaos is in order. Of course, the classical scientists knew that chaos existed, but religious and scientific dogma prevented them from doing much with it. Newton himself tried to discount chaotic influence in the solar system by proving its stability (which remains unproven to this day). Henri Poincaré won a prize in 1889 proving that previous scientists, Newton and Laplace among them, had failed to prove the stability of the solar system. In the process he invented several new branches of mathematics: dynamical systems theory, differential topology, global analysis, and qualitative dynamics, along with the theories of chaotic attractors and bifurcations (Abraham, 1994). To solve some of the math problems required millions of computations, so the actual application of this new math had to wait for the invention of the computer to quickly work the iterations of the problems. The first ap-plication of chaos math was done by Edward Lorenz in his study of the weather (Lorenz, 1963). I recommend James Gleick's Chaos: Making a New Science (1987) for the full story. Chaos theory directs a scientific study of the metapatterns of nature. Metapattern means a pattern of patterns, a "pattern that connects" diverse elements across space (disciplines, species, cultures, etc.) and time (evolution of life, ideas, civilization, etc.) (Bateson, 1979). Metapatterns identify self similarities across the boundaries of explicate reality. They lead the way back to the implicate order. Chaos scientists have learned that while chaos in nature is unpredictable, it is determined. Chaotic systems are not random. According to Julien Sprott (1993), a researcher of plasma physics and nonlinear dynamics, "chaos theory reconciles our intuitive sense of free will with the deterministic laws of nature;" chaotic systems "follow rules, but even simple rules can produce extreme complexity." What makes for the transition, the sudden radical change from order to chaos or chaos to order? As scientists explored the new territory of chaos, a fascinating discovery was made. At the frontier or edge between chaos and order, neither entirely dissolving into chaos nor settling into stable order, were the processes of dynamic systems. At a certain point of complexity between chaos and order, systems became spontaneously self organizing. Such systems are called complex, and the study of them is the new science of complexity (Bak, 1996; Bar–Yam, 1997; Brown and Novick, 1983; Çambell, 1993; Capra, 1996; Casti, 1994; Cohen and Stewart, 1994; Gell–Mann, 1994; Lewin, 1992; Mainzer, 1996; Mitchell,2009; Sabelli, 1989; Waldrup, 1992; Walnum, 1993; and Williams, 1997). As a metascience, complexity theory has been taken up across disciplines by many fields—biology (Dean, 1997; Kelso, 1995), computer science (Holland, 1995, 1998), economics (Peters, 1994), history (Abraham, 1994), meteorology (Lorenz, 1993), organizational development (Stacy, 1996; Wheatley, 1994), psychology (Mahoney, 1991; Van Eenwyk, 1997)—in other words, any field which studies systems. In the simplest terms, a system is a set of causes that combine to produce a result (Flynn, 2001). It must be remembered that chaos and complexity theories are not yet "sciences." They form a loose structure of intense scientific exploration along many fronts. While chaotic systems abound, actually determining the specific qualities of chaos and its presence is difficult. Furthermore, the mathematics to describe chaotic and complexity processes is still being developed. There is not even an agreed upon explicit definition of complexity. And the processes of complexity are named differently by different theorists, who must come up with something to call what they study. At this point, it is not even clear which theory, chaos or complexity, is the part and which the whole. The advantage of complexity and chaos theories is that they provide a language and imagery better than any theories before them to explain what it is that "leads to predictability (similarities) and uncertainty (dissimilarities) with regard to behavioral, social, and cultural outcomes" (Dean, 1997). They help explain "the vast diversity and the universal similarities which exist between individual people, societies, and cultures" (Dean, 1997). Cultural differences aside, according to Alan Dean (1997) "it can be asserted with confidence that no two individuals will experience the external world in exactly the same way." Even though identical twins raised separately share remarkable similarities, they still generate different outcomes. In the rest of this chapter and throughout the book, I will present how chaos and complexity theories inform our sense of being human in the world. These theories help us understand how one abused child might become an abusing adult while another equally abused sibling might not. Or how one intervention can work with one depressed person and not with another. This is for several reasons. First, human beings and all their doings are complex dynamical systems, thus subject to sensitivity to initial conditions. No two people are ever going to begin any process in life identically, and very small differences in initial input can result in very large differences in later outcomes. Second, people are not merely passive recipients of external forces; they create their own environments (Plomin, 1994). Third, intelligence generates the causes of its own behavior: "once intelligence has evolved in a species, then thereafter brains have a causal force equal to that of genes" (Plotkin, 1994). Fourth, the exercise of intelligence generates changes in neurophysiological structures during an individual's lifetime in response to experience (Edelman, 1992). It may seem to devalue our humanity to describe human beings as complex systems like all other complex systems in the universe. However, it is the complexity dynamic that makes for the extraordinary diversity of people. Every person is a generator of unique self organization and the outcome is the intensely personal mythology that is lived by each one of us.

Dynamic Change and Healing

When complexity sciences talk about the short term unpredictability and long term consistency of complex dynamic systems, it is helpful to remember that we human beings are complex dynamic systems, as are our families, work groups, villages, towns, cities, states, nations, and the international community. While a complex system is unpredictable, there are certain parameters of importance:

1. Short term change is frequently over estimated. 2. Long term change is frequently underestimated. 3. The more specific the prediction, the less likely it is to be correct. It is safer to predict that marriages that cannot handle aggression will end in divorce than it is to say that Bob and Mary, who cannot fight constructively, will divorce. 4. Past performance is an undependable predictor of future results. 5. The most reliable predictions are those that follow established trends. Predictions follow basins of attraction. If we can identify the qualities and geography of the strange attractor of a dynamic system, we can anticipate the flow of that system but not the specific emergent changes. 6. If a person's, couple's, or group's behaviors are generally predictable, there is or will be a problem sooner or later. Human beings are complex dynamic systems for which general predictability is uncharacteristic. —Adapted from Robert X. Cringely's "The Five Rules of Prognostication" (1998) The complex dynamic system is designed to be remarkably adaptive at the same time that it has consistency and identity over time. This is why such a system is actually easier to control that a stable, simpler one. We are not generally bouncing off the pricks and arrows of fortune like a linear pinball in a machine. We are replete with checks and balances (like depression or shock) to prevent such disruptions. And if this becomes too stable, we have been gifted with boredom and curiosity to stir things up. Yet the case of Patty Hearst, who was kidnapped by and turned into a gun wielding member within a week of the Symbionese Liberation Army, shows that rapid chaotic change of the whole identity is possible. On a larger level, stable families can be thrown into chaos at weddings or funerals, times when membership of the system is disrupted. By the same token, chaotic, "dysfunctional" families can spontaneously generate emergent order under the same conditions. Even internationally, the end of the cold war and the complete breakup of the Soviet Union is another example of sudden transformation. Healthy human beings and human systems are operating optimally in the complexity groove and when they do they are remarkably resilient. When a person breaks into chaos we need to be careful, returning them to stability, then to optimal com-plexity.

When that person is stuck in a stability rut, on the other hand, carefulness can be counterproductive. We need to push them up into complexity, sometimes by way of a little controlled chaos, as in a healing ritual or psychodrama. When randomness strikes a complex dynamic system it can create new directions in which the system can grow. The "fluctuation, randomness, and unpredictability at the local level, in the presence of guiding or self referential principles, cohere over time into definite and predictable form" (Wheatley, 1994). If order is for free, then we do not have to be the orderers, struggling for control of reality. Instead of striving for control, order, and safety, we can seek the chaos in a system. We can intentionally nudge a person (family or group) to the edge of chaos and into the complexity space. We can save our ordering and controlling for when the client needs it because he or she is flooded into random chaos (due to a sudden death of a loved one, post traumatic shock, or psychosis, for example). We know that a person's self system is periodic when the same thing happens over and over again regularly. We know it is chaotic when a small stimulus produces a huge outcome, like falling in love at first sight. Or, conversely, when a huge stimulus produces a small outcome, like a rape resulting in obsessive or depressive or denying behavior in the victim. Pathology, argues John Briggs (1992), may be viewed as a loss of the "natural" background chaos in the mind or body. Or, conversely, it can be seen as an increase in the random chaos, exceeding the boundaries of the complex dynamic system's capacity to handle deterministic chaos. When the balance shifts too far in the direction of order, certain kinds of heart attacks, epileptic seizures, depression, or some self destructive habit may emerge; aspects of the system become phase–locked. On the other hand, too much random chaos can produce chronic fatigue syndrome, psychosis, or dissociative identity disorder. I believe that humans naturally have multiple personalities, part personalities, and roles (a life time of introjects transmuted into selfness). Dissociative identity disorders occur when the interlocking web of feedback among the multiple parts breaks down (or never got established). In summary, pathology could be described as "dysfractional." On a personal scale, we can help people process feelings by moving them from the linear expression of blame or complaint to the nonlinear expression of anger or grief. We can help them toward more powerful decision–making, given the quantum power of intentionality and focused observation of reality that creates new realities. All decisions put the stability of a self system at risk in some way. The image of a bifurcation attractor is very much like that of a decision tree. Too many options results in a move from deterministic to random chaos, as you can see in the bifurcation chart to the left (from Liebovitch, 1998), where X equals time and the bottom line, B, equals choices. The single line, the fixed point attractor of a possible choice, arises at 2.90 or so as the B line. The choice emerges at the B=3.00 value where it represents a period two attractor. Somewhere between 3.40 and 3.50 on B the bifurcation reaches a period four attractor (often the best time to decide). After another period doubling (now a period eight attractor) the onset of chaos begins, and at B=3.569946, the chaos of possibilities fills the phase space. When the time to decide arrives: we will do it (1) or we will not (2). At the next doubling, the period four attractor, the next choices, whatever the content of the decision, involve doing it (1) and liking it (3) or not liking it (4) or not doing it (2) and liking it (5) or not liking it (6). We have jumped from two choices (1 and 2) to four (3, 4, 5, and 6). At the next bifurcation there are eight choices, none as clear cut as before. There are still windows of opportunity for choices (indicated by the "white" in the phase space) that pop up, but mostly there is confusion. Most people who struggle with choices take too long to make a decision and need help to move from random chaos back to complexity (deterministic chaos).

Some avoid conscious choices altogether, letting their lives happen to them, more or less. They will hold off making plans for Friday Night until the last minute (in case something better comes along, i.e., the "right" decision). Others choose quickly between the "either" or the "or" and hope they can live with the result. Yet others go to the period four attractor and evaluate the pros and cons of doing and not doing and then make a choice. More miss the point and move into chaos. The missing link is often knowing wants, without which "real" choice is near impossible. We all strive for equilibrium in our lives. What constitutes equilibrium will be unique to each person, determined by their genetics, their history, and the vagaries of their personal mythologies, the meanings they generated to explain their most important experiences. The personal mythology is a powerful strange attractor that helps us know needs, identify wants, recognize alternatives, and evaluate them consciously before we plunge into chaos. As we make more evaluated choices—not an easy task—we engage in the Class IV system of choosing available to conscious beings. We participate in deterministic chaos which can lead to entirely new order, thus resetting a new, more complex level and state of equilibrium. The human dynamic system is pushed to complexity by the degree of choice available to each person as determined by their personal narrative autobiography. Each real choice is a bifurcation attractor that moves through awareness of choices of simple complication at the period two attractor to the doorway to complexity of the period four attractor. Simple choices lead to small predictable changes; complex choices lead to unexpectedly large effects. Rene Thom, who developed topological catastrophe theory, generated seven strange attractors he called catastrophe surfaces (Thom, 1975). He was interested in showing the lay of the land, so to speak, of endogenous (i.e., psychological) factors internal to societies and their members. One of his catastrophe surfaces is another look at bifurcation. Equilibrium is a fixed point attractor. When two equilibrium levels exist at the same time and are held by the same state variable—for example, any choice point—the catastrophe surface is a cusp or, colloquially, a "sheet with a pleat." This is a different picture of the effect of choice, one depicting the cumulative effect of choices by members of a whole social group.

4

Development A Complex Dynamic System

The implicate order is an undivided wholeness in flowing movement, a state of unending flux of enfoldment into the implicate wholeness and unfoldment out to the explicate order (Bohm, 1980). Entities unfolding from the implicate order are bound by a force of overall necessity as they enter the world of classical physics. This "force of overall necessity" is found, for example, in human development. Our biology can be seen as one of the sources of movement around the healing circle; it moves us through life in cycles. Like the turn of the seasons, this biological force of necessity can be seen as a template for our psychological cycles. In fact the healing circle is an archetype of the developmental template that is genetically programmed in each human being. Development is both linear and complex (Thelen, 1992). Thus, while the vicissitudes of nature and nurture are mediated by the dynamics of self organizing complexity, the biologically determined developmental timeclocks unfold for each of us, and their effects are replicated throughout each of our lives. They are a force of necessity. The evolution of the human brain that is capable of self referencing transcends the purely biological. Self referencing guides our psychological development and leads to the self organization of personal myths that script our lives. The biological actuality of human development in the explicate order anchors in time the personal myths and supporting rituals (subjects of coming chapters) of the time-liberated implicate order. It is our self referencing (our capacity for looking at the patterns of our lives for example) that allows us to actively reconstruct the outcomes of the developmental process, changing our personal myths and thus our lives. We become co?evolvers of the complexity of our own self?system, liberating ourselves from the arrow of time and linear cause and effect. We intentionally enter the complex state between chaos and order described in the last chapter. We step into recurring states of disequilibrium (chaos) and equilibrium (order) in human development, and by doing so, we can initiate new patterns of thought, feeling, wanting, or doing. The last chapter prepared us to see the self as a set of complex processes that leave a fractal record reflecting self?similarity at every scale. In this chapter I hope to show that we can see more about human development by viewing it as a complex state than has been possible within the traditional dualisms such as that of mind and body. Classical science focuses on the particular, thus breaking reality into many specialized disciplines. Complexity theory is a meta-theory. It focuses on the self-similarity in complex dynamic systems. Thus disciplinary boundaries do not prevent the meaningful association of similarities across these boundaries. This break with dualistic thinking is significant for understanding states of expanded consciousness and further discussion in later chapters on the efficacy of ritual in producing spontaneity and change.

Development is both a set of processes, operating within varying parameters and instigated by multiple causes, and a set of outcomes. Biological development is an unfolding dance of organisms whose genetic possibilities interact with and receive feedback from their environment over time. In spite of the arrow of time, there is a bi?directionality to development that encourages us to think that the past has not passed. Indeed, the regressions, repetitions, and recyclings of outcomes back to their initial conditions or beginnings are a common feature of most psychotherapies. It does not take much self–referencing to agree with Edna St. Vincent Millay that "it's not true that life is one damn thing after another?it's one damn thing over and over" (source unknown). The healing potential of recycling is particularly apparent in the design of human bonding. Human attachment seems to be innate and biologically determined. Yet it combines with feedback from our experiences of living to become a truly unique map of our capabilities for loving. Often that map leads us down the same relationship roads. On the other hand, as robust as the attachment pattern of childhood are throughout our lives, the are open systems, and thus open to changes. For example, the complementary processes to infant attachment behaviors are the care–giving behaviors of the first significant other. Caregiving is a different set of behaviors triggered by the attachment seeking ones. Thus a caregiver's attachment deficits can be healed through the giving of care. There is a way out of the "over and over." From the point of view of outcomes, development is "a progressive series of changes that occurs in a predictable pattern as the result of an interaction between biological (nature) and environmental (nurture) factors" (Salkind, 1985). According to their complexity of being, living creatures share in exploratory behavior and learning which affects the process of their development. Thus there are aspects of our being, activated by the very process of living, which take us beyond our genetically coded biological time clocks.

Human Development

In the last century, especially in the last fifty years, the unfolding of human beings from conception to death has been studied closely. Moreover, the increase in longevity has demanded studies in aging and life span development. Especially interesting has been data made possible by new technology for studying brain development of babies as they are exposed to experiences. Time Magazine (February 3, 1997) featured an article by Madeline Nash reviewing studies in infant development which assert that "the debate that engaged countless generations of philosophers?whether nature or nurture calls the shots?no longer interests most scientists. They are much too busy chronicling the myriad ways in which genes and the environment interact." Patterns of self-similarity have been observed. Human beings, given enough safety and freedom, seek to find their highest level of functioning. In the interaction between the natural endowment and the personal history, the first three years are the most important. In brain development, the first year is most important. By age two, the child's brain contains twice as many synapses and consumes twice as much energy as the brain of a normal adult. Brain growth draws to a close around the age of ten, and by age eighteen, the brain has declined in plasticity but increased in power by ruthlessly destroying its weakest synapses, preserving only those that have been tempered by experiences (Time, February 3, 1997). There are biologically timed windows of opportunity for growth and development connected by periods of consolidation. Furthermore, this development is multi–faceted. David Stern (1985) has already identified around a hundred lines of development, each having its own developmental story. Until recently, Western thought has tended to conceptualize development as linear. In truth, it is both linear and circular, as we shall soon see. Human growth processes are observed to be "seasonal" and to be replicated and recycled redundantly (Carter and McGoldrick, 1988; Levin, 1988: Levinson, 1978). Neither parents nor babies being perfect, all humans endure traumatic events from birth on throughout the life cycle. In their quest for fulfillment, humans store developmentally impinging trauma (in forgotten memories, in their bodies, in their habits, in their dreams, waking and sleeping) and continually seek conditions from later environ-mental conditions to reconnect with earlier development failures in order to set them right (Fromm and Smith, 1989). Human development is both an ongoing process and a progress toward distinct levels. On the whole it is a complex dynamic system, comprising many complex dynamic systems, yet some aspects of development are determined linearly. Developmental markers lead us to talk about these levels as steps of development. Four principles govern the developmental steps: 1. Several lines of development may occur simultaneously, but they each progress according to a biological time clock and through the same steps. 2. Each step, while having its own particular characteristics, contains elements of each of the others. 3. Each step is sequentially built upon the one before it. 4. A problem in one step is carried over into the others, but developmental momentum may obscure problems until later recycling.

The steps of development are a stairway to continued recyclings of nurturance, intruding, challenging, and structuring during the interactions between the primary caregiver and the child. I want to emphasize the undervalued cyclical nature and the related recycling of our "initial conditions" in early development. The force of biological necessity that develops stage upon stage while retaining self–similarity to those early conditions moves us around the Healing Circle. Our development repeats itself with variations. Our beginnings also suggest why viewing life as a cycle can lead to healing. Where we repeat our initial conditions we have the opportunity to intervene in them, to start over. Our "pathologies" can be paths toward fuller consciousness. In the careful and long?term research into the development of human beings from birth through adulthood that has been going on for the last fifty years, we are now beginning to identify numerous categories of development (Aimes et al, 1979; Brazelton, 1990, 1992; Burkes and Rubenstein, 1979; Erikson, 1980, 1982; Gould, 1978; Greenspan and Greenspan, 1985; Kagan, 1988; Kaplan, 1978, 1984; Karen, 1994; Klaus and Kennell, 1976; Konner, 1991; Krueger, 1989; Levin, 1988; Levinson, 1978; Mahler, 1975; Mahoney, 1991; Masterson, 1985; Miller, 1983; Piaget, 1981; Piaget and Inhelder, 1963; Small, 1998; Stern, 1977, 1985; Thomas and Chess, 1968; Wade, 1996; and Winnecott, 1987). Four general categories, Adaptive Behavior, Language Behavior, Motor Behavior, and Social Behavior, settle into the four quadrants of the Healing Circle. On the next two pages are four circular views of various dimensions of the development of humankind as they are related to these four general categories. These charts are arranged on the pages so that the categories are in their quadratically defined places (imagine a large circle around the book, with the binding as the vertical axis and a horizontal axis separating the two upper from the two lower charts). These charts are intended to represent the complexity of human development. You may find it easier to take in the significance of this variety by focussing on one quadrant or even one pointing arrow (they are arranged in approximately the same places on each circle) to see how each category unfolds. These charts depict the first five years around the circle. Whether we regress or progress, echoes of these behaviors appear throughout our lives.

5

Quadratic Process

Working with the Complexity of the Personal Mythology God is an intelligible sphere, whose center is everywhere and circumference nowhere. Quadratic Process A human being is a system comprised of systems. Selfsimilarity can be seen at every scale from our DNA to our bad habits. Consider the quartered circle. It is a set of four, like so many other biological, physical, and intuitive forms in the universe. The division into four creates the possibility of representing relationships of complementarity such as the seasons and our own DNA. It is an ancient symbol for representing the complex dynamic system of the seasons and the seasons of life. Indigenous cultures assumed the natural and human life cycle were related and even in our contemporary world, literature, philosophy, spiritual traditions and even secular life continues to represent human life in relation to seasonal metaphors. Our personal mythologies include implicit and explicit memory, the autobiographical narrative, attachment patterns, defensive patterns, and feedback from the environment. They are personal because each person generates one, and they are mythological because they are a vehicle for making meaning of our experience rather than a record of events. The self similarity of the developing mind is demonstrated in the emerging personal mythology. Quadratic process refers to the way humans live their lives in terms of the deep structure of reality. The quartered circle has represented this structure. A human life unfolds through a co–streaming of innate traits and external factors, and each life is unique. Yet we can isolate the patterns of that streaming—the rough turbulences, the dead ended eddies, the smooth flows, the dry beds.

Cycles of Healing, Cycles of Life

Human beings are an interface between consciousness and reality. To the degree that we become mindful of this interface, we participate in our own unfolding and with that of the unfolding universe. Any intention to observe our being with others, a reality, or ourselves is a spiritual act. In exercising consciousness we become co–creators of the unfolding complexity of life. Self reference appears to be built into development. Somewhere around fifteen years old, the human being's brain becomes capable of abstract math and self reference (Piaget, 1981). The awakening of self reference is the beginning of any psychic growth. To look at ourselves is to grow—even if we try not to change anything. The observer effect teaches us that the very act of looking at ourselves changes us. Self reference is the capacity for the subject to look at itself as an object. Of course, the part that is looking is still a subject, so complete objectivity is never possible. Self reference is a challenging task. Each act of self observation requires the creation of a new observer. Because we are experiencing a complementarity, holding the line between one and the other is difficult and frequently trance inducing. We usually need instruction to self reference well. Teaching self reference is one of the primary functions of many therapies. Self reference as it is configured by the Healing Circle is a spiritual discipline, connecting us to the implicate order. Objectivity and Subjectivity comprise one of those elementary complementaries, like wave and particle, that slip us into the fundamental nature of quantum reality like a floating leaf entering the mainstream of a river. The Healing Circle assists in self reference by mapping the surround. Like a compass it guides us to where our half–lives lie and where we are in our journeys around the full cycle of life. It holds the subject position while we look at our lives as objects. Making Changes Some changes in our lives are like stones dropped into the still pool of self. By these we can then measure the ripple effect of the changes across the whole life space we inhabit. According to the vision of reality developed by quantum physics, we have a lot to do with the measures we experience. Consciousness creates reality by observing it. The act of observation is a measure in itself. If we add hopes, dreams, desires, intentions, plans, implementations, and the stuff of human living, the measurements get much more complex. We are creatures of complexity. We not only live on the edge between chaos and order; we need to live there to live fully. Healthy people seem to create stress if their lives are too easy. Without reaching the zone of complexity, our lives lack the rich self organizations that emerge, and our vitality is subsequently diminished. The Healing Circle enables us to see the recyclings of our personal mythologies. Our personal mythologies are formed out of initial conditions, or our early development. The Healing Circle is a template for identifying the missing complementaries of our self organization and for directing us toward greater complexity and possibilities for living. Rather than a model for discovering pathology, it is a compass for identifying the missing parts of the whole life we might be living through proactive creativity. The use of the Healing Circle generates different kinds of questions and directs the attention of both the therapist and the client in particular ways. What is missing from the whole cycle in a particular individual's story—needs, wants, doing, or thinking? Or nurturance, intimacy, competence, or solid thinking? Or protection, permission, potency, or permanence? Or spring, summer, fall, or winter? What is he or she good at? What does an individual struggle most with and how does he or she usually compensate for this lack? Together therapist and client deduce the personal mythology and search out the missing half–life, co–creating a fuller personal mythology that feeds back into the initial conditions to bring about deep change in the whole system. I had a client, Robert, who seemed to get nowhere in his life. He was a therapist himself, with a small practice that would not grow. Robert was a hard working man who felt unwanted and abandoned by his parents. He seldom asked for help, and usually did not recognize his need for any. After several months of working together and clarifying that Robert had no idea what he wanted out of life, I noticed that he usually sat with his hands clenched.

Upon questioning, he discovered that he was unaware that he did this, but when he unclenched his hands he felt anxious. My mind flooded with explanations and psychological rationales for this behavior. Remaining silent, however, I got up and grabbed a handful of birdseed I keep in my office to feed Bird, my companion parrot. I approached Robert and asked him to hold out his hands, which he did: clenched. I spilled the seeds onto his clenched hands, and as they fell all over the floor I said: "These are the seeds of all the possibilities in your life." He burst into tears (a first) and buried his face in his (open) hands. In subsequent sessions he began speaking of things he wanted in his life—with unclenched hands and trepidation. Within six months his practice had doubled and he was preparing for a long desired vacation to Costa Rica. In a year he successfully terminated therapy. This was an intervention that sprang from Robert's personal mythology of abandonment. To avoid the pain of abandonment, Robert learned early to have few needs and to fend for himself. "After all," he would iterate, "who else is going to?" Keeping his needs small and his dreams dimmed, Robert lived a tidy life with few complications: No debts, no pets, and no loved ones. What was missing for Robert was any sense of a higher purpose in life, passion for anything, and connection to other people. When I saw his clenched hands, I immediately understood how he could have so little in life. How could he grab for anything that he wanted with his hands in knots? How could he want anything? Robert was clear that the fear when his hands were open was that he would lose whatever he got by reaching out for it. Most of us live half-lives, experiencing the same cycle over and over again. The use of the Healing Circle to identify our quadrants of deepest wounding can thus point to the complementary experiences we need to practice. The Healing Circle also brings into relief the entrances and exits to the transitional phases at which deep changes in our personal mythologies can happen. The Healing Circle facilitates eclectic therapeutic practices, bringing into view the need for a complex approach to consciousness because it is itself a complex system.

The essence of what I term the quadratic process is remarkably simple. It is rare that people seeking assistance will come with a clear and obvious need, emotional depth, unambivalent wants, clear objective perceptions of their behavior, and a sense of the meaning of their problem. In these cases, an immediate intervention can be made. However, in my experience, usually some cycles around the healing circle will be necessary. At the very least, the healer will help clients see how the parts of their personal mythology that they are aware of are related. Moreover, the healer can expose the client to the encrypted complementaries of their awarenesses such as the overfunctioning that is typically complementary to undernurturing or the angry righteousness that defends against the fear of betrayal. Awakening relationships between complementaries reconnects the explicate to the implicate, the part to the whole, and in doing so alters consciousness, increases energy and plants a foot in each universe. Once you get the idea of the dynamics of the system, using the Healing Circle to extrapolate the personal mythology is actually pretty easy. Some guidelines for using it as a metamodel for therapy are useful. Because the Healing Circle addresses the complementarity of the explicate and implicate orders of existence, it resists reductionistic processes and simple cause and effect thinking. Few things are as they seem when it comes to understanding and healing humankind. When we are dealing with the profundity of human existence, the opposites of profound truths may be more profound truths. The Tree of Human Life is a dynamic complex system with roots in the implicate order. Identity and the Self Before going on, I want to clarify the models of identity and self that my use of quantum physics, complexity theory and the healing circle assume. Establishing identity is one of the main outcomes of a personal mythology. Identity is established when we measure our experiences by creating meaning for them. Identity is not nearly so firm as we would like to believe. As with Patty Hearst, our identity can be swept away easily by cruelty, deprivation, and isolation, punctuated by moments of connection.

Identity is a mid–level magnification of what I call the Soul Fractal, the highest level. Identity is a self organizing fractal that brings our various roles to consciousness as a coherent whole. Identity might be thought of as the image reflected by the still waters of the self. It is not the self. The self is an even larger complex system that includes identities. The process of developing the self is the work of our lifetimes, and shifting identities are the stepping stones through the stream of time toward the stillness of eternity. J. L. Moreno felt that the soul, a higher level of magnification than identity, was not the beginning but rather the end of evolution. He theorized that an infant entered the world undifferentiated from that state. Yet this world was the matrix of identity from which the self and its branches, the identities, and their branches, the roles, emerged in gradual stages, as explicate emerges from implicate. Generally, these roles emerge developmentally, beginning with the psychosomatic and ending with the social. He distinguished three classes of roles: Psychosomatic: (physiological) roles, like the eater or the sleeper Psychodramatic: (psychological) roles, like ghosts, demons, or heroes Social: like parent, plumber, or healer. Self examination and/or therapy help us track the emergence of psychodramatic and psychosomatic roles. Often the most difficult issues are embedded in the initial conditions of the complex, dynamic system. Thus eating or sleep disorders, for example, are extremely challenging to get to the beginning of and change. We are generally most conscious of the emergence of our social roles as they are marked by rites of passage.

As roles develop overlapping behaviors with one another, they integrate into a unit, a kind of partial self. Eventually, operational links develop among the three classes of roles and they form a unit of identity. An identity is a fractal record of the emerging complex system of the self. As physics has explained, subatomic particles join to make atoms, atoms join to make molecules, molecules join to make organic and inorganic matter, and objects join to make systems of all kinds, ultimately universes. Similarly, out of smaller clusters of psychosomatic, psychodramatic, and social roles larger sub–identities emerge at the edge between the chaos of the undifferentiated universe and the soul. These clusters of sub–identities self organize as an individual tries new behaviors and lives with the intention to complete him or herself. Action precedes selfhood. The self is an individually developed construct generated by personal choices with all the attendant bifurcations, personal experiences (and their "measurements" into meaning), and the complex dynamic system of the human mind. I envision that the self is a complex, dynamic system of nested interlocking identities. The Soul Fractal may be an eternal complex, dynamic energy system of interlocking selves, sequentially entering and exiting time from birth to death to rebirth. Self referencing would then be a function of that self of the Soul Fractal which is in time. Perhaps we journey from the implicate order of reality to the explicate order and back again, cycling through cosmic seasons.

While the Healing Circle can be used to explore any level of magnification of the Soul Fractal, most of the time we have a narrow focus. We generally prefer one identity or sometimes a particular role within our own personal mythologies, blocking our own access to further identities or roles. Recognizing the unlived complementaries of our personal mythologies is the first step toward change and the many possibilities of the self. The personal mythology contains them all. Quadratic Process: Plexing the Personal Mythology The Healing Circle can be seen as a model based upon trauma to the developmental process. Our personal mythologies emerge from the effects of our experiences on our development. While events and genetics have an effect, "relationships early in life may shape the very structures that create representations of experience and allow a coherent view of the world: Interpersonal experiences directly influence how we mentally construct reality" (Siegel, 1999). I have argued that human beings are complex dynamic systems and therefore we are heavily influenced by the initial conditions of our lives. Research demonstrates that during the first few years, the most important development is that of the brain. Our first relationships and the emotions generated by them directly effect the development of the brain into what some now call mind. According to the Healing Circle, if as newborns our environment is filled with chaos, dangerous parental inconstancy, or is absent of meaningful structures to internalize, we can develop a mythology of meaningless. Or if our caregiver's are unable to bond with us, are mis- or unattuned, or neglect us, we can develop mythologies of abandonment. As we enter the world of language and growing independence and mobility, our caregivers may be unable to mirror us, may consistently break their word with us, or may be more focused on what they want for us rather than helping us learn about our own wants. We can develop mythologies of betrayal. And finally, our caregivers may over- or undersupport our emergent competency in the world, or they may even shame or humiliate our attempts at doing things. This can lead to personal mythologies of powerlessness. Of course, if we are exposed to extreme trauma at any time in our lives, trauma that undermines our belief in our world or ourselves,

we may overlay a meaningless myth upon an already existing one. Ordinarily, as our early development cycle recycles without intervention throughout our lives, we continue to bypass the developmental stages that were lost to trauma. Experience seems to verify the personal mythology we have created, because the myth frames the reality that we are living. So to begin plexing the personal mythology, I assign names to the major movements of the life flow. The Home Base is the quadrant of behaviors that we revert to under stress. The Starting Point is the last successful stage on the path of development before derailment and, therefore, usually a safe place to begin the healing process. Ground Zero is the complementary quadrant to the Home Base and is the indicator of a chronological site of early childhood injury to the self. Because the person escaping the stress of traumatic injury by fleeing to the complementary quadrant completely misses the next quadrant, that quadrant is called the Doorway. It holds unexplored possibilities for the self. Here are more complete definitions of the four quadrants of quadratic process. Depending on the trauma, as you will see in just a few pages, the Home Base will vary. The other three configure around the Home Base.

Patterns of Impasse

Now we will explore the patterns of impasse implicated by the Healing Circle. Just as the Celtic eightfold year (King, 1994) articulates eight gates of passage, so the Healing Circle has eight patterns of impasse. These impasses are moments of self measurement. One of the many analogues to life from quantum physics (Herbert, 1985), the pinhole effect, occurs when electrons are shot through a pinhole to be recorded on a phosphor screen. When the pinhole is larger, the electrons are recorded as particles. But when the iris of the pinhole is constricted, an act of measurement occurs and the phosphor screen records the concentric rings of their wave function. Getting squeezed through a knothole may be a great doorway to the implicate order. In life, we organize our thoughts, feelings, wants and behaviors to have a "particular" experience of our reality and ourselves. In therapy, as in life, when the constraints (the pinhole) through which we birth our selves are constrained even more, we eventually reach the possibilities of the wave pattern of the implicate order. At the maximum optimal constraint, we are illuminated. Of the eight patterns of impasse, there is one for each of the four seasons of the quartered circle, called patterns of ricochet, and there is one for each of the four directions, called patterns of reversal. Your personal mythology will determine which of the patterns are easy and which are difficult. These eight patterns fit around the quartered circle, the ricochets on the inside and the reversals at the axis points around the outside. Here is the map of the patterns:I argued that human consciousness is a self organizing complex dynamic system. The quartered circle is a linearized template of the Healing Circle, a self organized complex dynamic system comprised of the millions of events of a human life.

The Change Process

Human beings are remarkably able to make do with the way things are. After all, at birth, we are one of the most adaptive species on the planet. Our prolonged dependency requires that we detect and respond to the needs and intent of our caretakers. If we succeed, we survive. Luckily we have a marvelous brain which grows phenomenally in the first two years of our lives. Our brains help us establish mind to mind links or inter subjectivity with our caregivers. By two, our brains have more capacity and possibilities that at any other stage of our lives. Unfortunately, not all caregiver environments are alike. Thus the remarkable ability to make do with the way things are. Things must get much worse, first before real change can begin. As creatures of habit (rather than instinct), we maintain remarkable denial in order to keep things the way they are. This is confirmed by complexity theory where a dysfunctional system must be perturbed into deterministic chaos in order for new order to emerge. Research into the change process shows that the positive elements for change increase regularly in relation to a regular decrease in the negative reasons for changing (Prochaska et al, 2002). In their book, Changing for Good, Prochaska and his colleagues state a Strong Principle of Change: from precontemplation of change to taking action for change requires a standard deviation increase in positive beliefs and reasons for making the change. Sometimes we must confront denial, thus generating even more resistance to change (negative reasons for changing) in order to create the conditions for real change to occur. Of course, people do come for help in a state of crisis. We must first calm and stabilize them. But this is not true change, as they merely return to the way things are. For real change to begin, we must gradually introduce controlled chaos back into their lives. The Axis Dance In applying the quadratic process, we must resist our lifelong training to think linearly and reductionistically. A very important consideration to remember is the remarkable creativity of human beings. We will turn conserves upside down and find the most unique ways to express ourselves. Unpredictable self organization is natural to us, given optimal conditions. We no sooner identify our core myths than we find exceptions. In truth, we all accumulate traumas in all four seasons of living. Nevertheless, when we seek help for the first time, we usually present problems and issues from our home base quadrant, the quadrant complementary to the core mythology, called ground zero. There may be a few issues from ground zero, but usually they have to be inferred, as the core myths are generally unconscious. During the mid therapy process, issues can come from any quadrant as the whole self is in transition. Healing is wholeness. If someone comes for help in mid therapy, it is difficult to determine the core mythology if he or she has not determined it already. At the end of therapy, issues emerge mostly from the ground zero, with a few from the home base, just the reverse of the beginning.

In the beginning of the therapy process, we often have to "dance on the axis." For example, a person with a core betrayal myth may seem like he or she has a chaos myth some of the time. Over time, by looking at the issues of the other quadrants, you can determine the true core mythology. A person with a betrayal mythology will have much better self– care and nurturing in his or her life than the person with the chaos mythology. Whereas the chaos person will enjoy challenges, the betrayed person dreads them, no matter how many achievements. Looking to the other axis, the abandoned or disempowered core myths, we solve the question, as before, by comparing the clients' behaviors in the other seasons of their lives. Thus someone with an abandonment myth will have much poorer intimate relationships than someone with a disempowerment mythology. In fact, these two often find one another because the strength of the disempowered person's intimacy skills make him or her the only one who can stand the hard driving abandoned ones, while the abandoned ones find their partners loveable in spite of their "uselessness." Sometimes the axis dance is what we see first. Regarding the "end" of therapy, most of us regress under stress to the original core mythology regardless of the amount of personal growth we have done. Nothing is ever lost; and we cannot be who we are not. However, changes that we have made to our personal myths direct alternative paths to spontaneous and timely recovery of grounded selfness. Differential Therapy By therapy, I mean the healing of the soul. Given optimal resources of time, money, intelligence, maturity, competence, creativity, reciprocity, love, knowledge, intuition, and so forth therapy is a long process. By differential, I do not mean simply different strokes for different folks. In the Healing Circle, we consider the ways that our differences are alike. Each human being is a complex dynamic system of dynamic systems. Each part of such systems effects the system. Changing one part does not do much. Change a few and the system enters deterministic chaos, where new order emerges for free. Change too many and you simply have random chaos—usually perceived as death. In applying the Healing Circle model, we must resist our lifelong training to think linearly and reductionistically. A very important consideration to remember is the remarkable creativity of human beings. We will turn conserves upside down and find the most unique ways to express ourselves. Unpredictable self-organization is natural to us, given optimal conditions. In truth, we all accumulate traumas in all four seasons of living. Nevertheless, when we seek help for the first time, we usually present problems and issues from our home base quadrant, the quadrant com-plementary to the core mythology, called ground zero. There may be a few issues from ground zero, but usually they have to be inferred, as the core myths are generally unconscious. During the mid therapy process, issues can come from any quadrant as the whole self is in transition. Healing is wholeness. If someone comes for help in mid therapy, it may be difficult to determine the core mythology if he or she has not determined it already. At the end of therapy, issues emerge mostly from the ground zero, with a few from the home base, just the reverse of the beginning. In the beginning of the therapy process, we often have to "dance on the axis." For example, a person with a core betrayal myth may seem like he or she has a chaos myth some of the time. Over time, by looking at the issues of the other quadrants, you can determine the true core mythology. A person with a betrayal mythology will have much better self– care and nurturing in his or her life than the person with the chaos mythology. Whereas the chaos person will enjoy challenges, the betrayed person dreads them, no matter how many achievements. Looking to the other axis, the abandoned or disempowered core myths, we solve the question, as before, by comparing the clients' behaviors in the other seasons of their lives. Thus someone with an abandonment myth will have much poorer intimate relationships than someone with a disempowerment mythology. In fact, these two often find one another because the strength of the disempowered person's intimacy skills make him or her the only one who can stand the hard driving abandoned ones, while the abandoned ones find their partners loveable in spite of their "uselessness." Sometimes the axis dance is what we see first. Regarding the "end" of therapy, most of us regress under stress to the original core mythology regardless of the amount of personal growth we have done. Nothing is ever lost; and we cannot be who we are not. However, changes that we have made to our personal myths direct alternative paths to spontaneous and timely recovery of grounded selfness.

Cycles of Growth: The Therapy Process

When we become conscious of what we are feeling, wanting, doing, and thinking, we shift from behaving ritualistically (habitually) to "doing ritual." For example, the person who is measuring him or herself by betrayal may be preoccupied with unemployment, divorce, or what have you, and generally so busy struggling with self and others that the sense of letting go of all previous self definitions and surrendering to a transformation is hardly present. If that sense can be engendered, usually by a healer/therapist figure (like Joseph Campbell on television), the person can participate in a rite of transformation and move on to the recovery room where, in isolation, he or she can integrate the new selfness. Therapy itself is a ritual. It involves responding to the call for change that comes to us in various ways: confrontation by our self defeating behaviors; exposure of some limiting belief about ourselves, others and/or the world; unexpressed or over–expressed feelings; or the decay, exhaustion,or death of a dream, vision, or plan for a life. We separate from the everyday mundane reality in our search for a healer/therapist, but we do not really enter the therapy process until we commit ourselves to observing ourselves fearlessly in all our ways. Self referencing is the key to shifting from the quasi–periodic system of the half–life to the wholeness and self organization of complexity. The "ordeal" of the therapy process begins with the identification of the underlying core personal myth(s) that drive(s) the unfolding of our lives. For example, let us take the client whose underlying core personal myth is one of betrayal, a wounding in the second quadrant of the Healing Circle. The overall therapy process requires a passage from the quadrant of wounding through the unaccessed half–life and then encountering one's complementary home base roles with new resources. The unaccessed half–life is the liminal phase of the ritual of therapy. It is the margin, the no man's land, where the changes to wholeness are accomplished. The protagonist, the journeyer of the therapy, must undergo a rite of separation. He or she must leave the fear, pain, and loss of betrayal as well as the protective alternation of his or her judgments. Then he or she encounters the challenges to a new life, a life without proving the family wrong, him or herself right—or to otherwise explain the world as unfolding from the big bang of betrayal. There may then proceed any length of time (usually longer than the client imagines or wants it to be) during which the protagonist of the therapy will learn the new behaviors of a new life—one not yet actually defined. Brief solution focused therapy is probably not properly called "therapy." Consulting is probably a better word. Furthermore, while effective and relatively cheap in the short run, in the long run, it may be counterproductive, particularly when the presenting problem (from the home base) is symptomatic of a need for a deeper level change (in ground zero). Therapy, which is about healing the soul, is blocked. The soul's urge to heal itself may present louder "calls to adventure," in short, worse problems. I will describe the process of therapy using the Healing Circle to achieve more wholeness. To heal is to arrive at a whole person integration of all our quadrants of living. This involves several steps (indicated by the numbered circles in the charts below). One must recognize home base as compensatory to ground zero. One must accept ground zero and learn to live in it in spite of anxieties arising out of fears of re–wounding. One must claim the territory of the doorway. Finally, one must encounter and integrate the home base roles and behaviors. There are four phases to Healing Circle therapy. Phase One (The Red Zone—0, 1, 2): The client is uncomfortable from time to time when the (1) home base behaviors do not work as well as usual or when the (0) ground zero generally unconscious experiences are triggered and discomfort rises up from within. But generally the client is able to engage in (2) starting point behavior enough to repress the discomfort. Mind you, the client may be totally conscious of the unfelt and thus unexperienced facts of trauma in his or her life. Therapy is sought for when the unfelt affect of this trauma seeks outlet. Most people enter therapy when life in the home base becomes intolerable. This can have numerous causes (usually simultaneous). For example, they can have a home base life style that is no longer viable. Or aspects of their core mythology may have surfaced in ways (too intense, too frequent) that they cannot stand. In any case they come for help. The therapist helps them get their life tolerably on track in the moment (1) and (2) begins to uncover the core mythology. Life disturbing concerns have priority, but the personal mythology holds supremacy. Phase Two (The Blue Zone—3, 4, 5): Phase Two begins when the client and therapist have a working hypothesis about the core personal mythology. Clients usually come to the therapy session uncomfortable and leave feeling better. Over and over the process will move from discomfort to comfort through identifying core elements of ground zero (0). If the client is receptive (and the therapist on the mark, of course), the therapy moves to Phase Two, self-referencing, by examining how life's problems are generated by the core mythology. The red rounds will happen over and over until the client begins to anticipate their occurrence in his life. Before therapy, these occurrences are recognized after the fact. In Phase Two, the client learns to recognize them while they are happening. Over time, the therapist has an idea, metaphor, or archetype about the ground zero and some guesses about how the wounding may have occurred. The therapist may or may not share these hypotheses with the client. Sharing these early usually does little good and can do harm. Instead, the therapist asks questions and makes interventions to test the hypotheses about the client's half–life. This is generally very powerful and the client becomes engaged in the process of self-discovery. In the beginning of the second phase, the client comes to therapy distressed and leaves relieved. As this phase matures, the client comes in calm and leaves distressed. This is a crucial time in the therapy. The client may lose heart and want to leave the process. This is a good time to share those hypotheses about the core mythology and traumatizing experiences. The therapist can also give homework to assure that the client is carrying the growth out into his community. This kind of arrangement can also give the therapist feedback regarding the nature of the support that the client has. Except for clients with abandonment mythologies, the therapist may recommend group at this time to help the client implement changes that are trying to emerge. Or the therapist may see a need to see the family or partner of the client in joint sessions. Telling the client about the nature and flow of the therapy process may also help at this point. Some clients will ask for this information. Some clients bring their learnings into a supportive family (or group) system, and the gains they experience there are enough to sustain them through these hard times. These clients move into Phase Three. Others reach a therapeutic plateau where, not feeling so miserable, they may leave therapy, at the end of Phase Two. If they do, their therapy is incomplete and they may return to therapy later. As Phase Two matures, the therapist engages the client at the starting point (2), that quadrant of living that the client has mastered, and each session involves a ritual healing in the ground zero trauma, a piece at a time. Phase two moves on to phase three when the client completes the rite of passage from the ground zero into the doorway (3). In Phase Three the client moves into the half–life that he has not yet lived in much and becomes comfortable there (3, 4, and 5). During this phase, issues will distribute throughout the quartered circle, and axis dancing is common. Crises will provoke regression. This is an excellent time for group work.

In addition to doing work around issues, some completely new, the client will also be learning new roles and behaviors for the new whole–life. In the first phase, the client experiences distress after a triggered event. In the second phase, the client experiences the triggering event and learns more about the trigger. In the third phase, the client anticipates triggers to the core mythology while discovering other trauma triggers the original core myth masked. Phase Three (The Green Zones—6, 7, 8, 9, 10): Phase three begins when the client encounters the old home base roles with wholeness. Eventually the client must make the rite of passage though the doorway from ground zero to the home base (where, to paraphrase T. S. Eliot, she will arrive where she started and know the place for the first time. This is generally a time of deep grief. Like all grief, it begins with denial of those former roles followed by anger. When the client has completed the grief work, the task of self-acceptance can begin. This is a time of great excitement, even joy. Clients with abandonment myths take the longest to leave therapy while clients with chaos myths will leave quickly. Some need help letting go, some need encouragement to slow down, take stock, and really appreciate their accomplishments. As you can see from the diagrams below, clients are encouraged to complete the cycle that they are on before their final rite of separation. It is important to remember that life is not linear. Nor is it circular. It is both. When you combine the line and the circle over time, you get the spiral. Life recycles in expanding or contracting spirals. What this means is that these passages, these threshold crossings, come up over and over. We may successfully cross over the first few times, then get bogged down as the demands of adult living become more complex. When we do, we will play out a ricochet or reversal pattern. These phase–locked patterns at worst are mechanistically determined, alternating periodic systems. At best, they are quasi–periodic. We have made the complexity of our lives linear again until we have the resources to strive for completion. The object of the Quadratic Process of the Healing Circle is to assist the client through the Doorway back into self organizing complexity.

. An actual infant/child (or anyone else facing a truly new threshold requiring a balancing of self-acceptance and new expectations of others) makes a self-limiting meaning of experiences that are too intense and/or complicated to be incorporated into memory, thus creating (or reinforcing) an archetypal pattern of response to any similar seeming experiences in living. 1. A client enters therapy because compensatory behaviors (overfunctioning and excessive "doings") are not working. 2. The client uses capacity to think and use of facts to approach healing abandonment trauma. 3. The client recognizes the abandonment as real and as unrelated to her/his personal worth and value and experiences feelings of despair, grief, self-love, worthiness, and any other feelings necessary for completeness. 4. The client experiences relationships reciprocally and intimately and without self-abandonment, thus permitting healthy separation from significant others. 5. The client experiences a new sense of personal empowerment in competence by doing things that matter to her/him personally. 6. The client encounters her/his "human doer" with love and acceptance, thus transforming her or his psyche. 7. The client experiences her/his former half-life with feelings, emotional consciousness, a sense of personal empowerment, self-confidence, thus loving and accepting her/himself in a new way. 8. The client encounters her/his abandoned self and contracts for constancy in self-care, thus balancing self-love and others expectations. 9. The now whole client completes rest of the cycle in healthy relatedness with self and others. 10. The client separates from the therapeutic process.

6

Healing Circle Compass

The chess board is the world; the pieces are the phenomena of the universe; the rules of the game are what we call the laws of Nature. The player of the other side is hidden from us. We know that his play is always fair, just, and patient. But we also know, to our cost, that he never overlooks a mistake, or makes the smallest allowance for ignorance.

The greatest challenge of our adult lives is to work through the inevitable traumas of our childhoods and to incorporate the resulting lost, dissociated fragments of self into our awareness of our reasons for being, wanting, doing, and believing. This largely unconscious story is called the personal mythology in the Healing Circle dialogue. Its underlying narrative thrust carries us like boats on a river to the unresolved and unincorporated experiences that shape its course. Each of us is hard wired to create a narrative autobiography that explains the reasons for our life paths and yet contains within it the hidden keys to what is missing. The recovery of lost or under-developed parts is the essence of all healing. Healing is arriving at Wholeness and it is a life long process of Completion. The Healing Circle maps a template of discovery that helps uncover this unconscious river of life. The rounded, feminine, holding circle joined with the angular, masculine, directional cross forms one of the oldest symbols of wholeness and unity generated by human kind. This symbol also represents the cycle of the seasons. When we add the two solstices and two equinoxes that separate the four seasons, they make up the eight key passages or gates of the quartered circle.

Ancient wisdom held that "as above, so below": thus our human lives unfolded seasonally also. The process of human development over the life span is easily correlated to the seasons. Early stages of our development are largely time driven, pushing us forward stage by stage whether we complete them or not. To grow a self, the newborn human's developmental template requires a spring like protective holding environment for all new beginnings, a fruitful harvest of meaningful connections to significant other(s) for emergent selfhood, a gradual challenging towards mastery of stage specific skills for developing independence, and a fluid modeling of new realities for incorporation of new meaning into our self awareness. Whether these requirements are optimally met stage by stage or not, the arrow of time keeps flying forward. The emerging self makes adjustments to get enough of what is missing or just to survive. These adaptations influence how further development unfolds. This, then, affects qualities of the template, thus influencing all future developmental sequences.

The Healing Circle identifies eight states or stations of development. In each, we are either developing and/or upgrading stage appropriate skills or we are dealing with a threshold crossing to a new set of stage appropriate skills. These passages are time and/or process driven. If all goes well enough (perfection can be traumatizing), we will turn cycle upon cycle in a rising spiral of development until our time comes to pass on to some other state of being. However, even when all is well, traumas will happen. These traumas create impasses that can block us from half the cycle of the circle until we heal them. Even when we have other contradictory traumatic experiences, our core impasses reframe our experiences to fit our story. These impasses are moments of self measurement (of our requisite skill sets) resulting in our personal mythologies. Our personal mythologies are activated under stress, and their sole purposes are to enhance our strengths and neutralize and preserve our underdeveloped potentials. At these stressful times, we organize our thoughts, feelings, wants and behaviors to have a "particular" experience of our reality and ourselves. All psychological theories must account for the repetition of behaviors (often self destructive) and the transformational changes and growth that are a part of being human. In the Healing Circle, these are explained by the concepts of recycling, derailments from the lifelong track of optimal, biologically driven developmental processes and stages, and the creative emergence of each person's personal mythology or narrative autobiography. Specific traumas or retraumatizations to specific developmental phases threaten us with anxiety or pain. Our brains protect us by making an instantaneous quantum leap to the life experiences represented by the complementary quadrant on the Healing Circle. For example, an infant is neglected and denied a protective holding environment (the Spring Quadrant). Her magnificent brain places her instantly in the mental state of meeting challenges to mastery (the Fall Quadrant) so that she can take care of herself and survive. In doing so, she by-passes half the cycle of experiences represented by the Healing Circle: Part of the protective holding environment, all of the meaningful connection to others, and part of the challenges to mastery become temporarily irrelevant. If the neglect is repeated, our abandoned baby girl or boy can develop a personal mythology of lovelessness, creating a narrative that emphasizes the half-life of doing for connection (part of the Fall Quadrant), thinking about and immersion in the details of explicit reality (all of the Winter Quadrant), and just enough self care to survive (part of the Spring quadrant).

This process can occur, of course, in any quadrant. Because the human brain takes so long to become fully functional and continues developing over the life span, it simplifies things by settling into a temporary half-life where all experiences are explained by the quadrant of most frequent or intense derailment. The experiences outside the half-life are encrypted in the personal mythology, available for later unpacking and incorporation.

In the Healing Circle view, the chronological site of the early traumatic derailments that form the organizing principle of the core myth is called Ground Zero, the Quadrant of Limiting (in this case, self care, self love, and self worth). Experiences here shape the narrative of our lives. The complementary quadrant of experiences our brains quantumly leap to when we are stressed is called the Home Base, the Quadrant of Overt Behavior (in this case, doing to become indispensable). Experiences here shape the history of our lives. Once relieved of distress, we can continue on the cycle, entering the fully lived in quadrant of the half-life, where we have access to the full repertoire of resources pertinent to the particular season of living. This is where we are most confident and where helpers can best reach us. It is called the Starting Point, the Quadrant of Accessible Resources (in this case, thinking and data collecting). In helping someone, we guide them by turning them to their Starting Point for resources. Then we engage with them in the Ground Zero trauma(s), over and over, and eventually explore missed experiences and develop missing skills. Next we facilitate a rite of passage (in this case, a rite of continuity) thus crossing the threshold between the Ground Zero Quadrant and the Doorway, the Quadrant of Discovery and New Resources (in this case, reciprocal open relations with trusted others). Optimally, we will continue our helping relationship with them as they cycle through this season with full awareness for the first time. If they experience a derailing trauma in this new life space (a distinct probability), they are likely to revert to their core myth and the familiar Home Base. With prompting we can often get them on track quickly. Eventually, they will require a second rite of passage, (in this case, a rite of separation) thus crossing the threshold between the Doorway Quadrant and the unfamiliar part of their Home Base. Here they can experience the missed experiences and develop missing skills so that they can cross the threshold between their Home Base and the Starting Point, as if for the first time, with new eyes, new feelings, new information, and new skills. They will have transformed their determined doing into purposeful action. For our abandoned baby, this is the path to wholeness and her or his true release from the Spell of Human Doing to the Richness of Human Being.

7

Stations of Development: The Eight Gates Recycled

Many traditions have used the segmented circle, called a mandala, to hold the complexity of living. Among some Native American tribes, for example, the Spider, who with her eight legs is the weaver of all the infinite possibilities of creation, renders the web of life. Her legs represent the eight gateways of spirit—the four winds of change and the four directions. In Tao of Chaos, Katya Walter (1998) demonstrates that the I Ching is essentially a complex dynamic system utilizing the same universal order of complementary chaos that DNA uses. The eight gates are represented by the eight trigrams of the "Old Family Mandala" of the I Ching (later expanded to sixty–four hexagrams by pairing the old family mandala with its counterclockwise cycle and then noting the unfolding progression of line by line changes). Of the eight gates, there are four patterns of ricochet, one for each of the four seasons of the quartered circle, and there are four patterns of reversal one for each of the four thresholds that separate them. The patterns of ricochet relate to the experiences myths are made of. I call this pattern a ricochet because when the trauma derails development at Ground Zero, the brain ricochets consciousness off at right angles into the opposite, complementary quadrant of the life experiences represented by the Healing Circle, carrying our narrative with it. This movement is instantaneous, a quantum leap. Patterns of ricochet arise out of blindness to possibilities. When our brains remove us instantly from perceived danger, we are prevented from learning the possibilities inherent in the missed experiences. Patterns of reversal arise out of resistance to possibilities. Patterns of reversal happen when we need to hold fast to our current core mythology rather than answer the call to cross a threshold into a new growth. Patterns of reversal occur because we are missing one or more of the essential skills needed to make the threshold crossing into the Doorway quadrant in the quadrant unlived half-life. The treatment is to identify the missing skill(s) and develop it so that we can cross the threshold. Our personal mythologies are robust defenses of our integrity and identity. Readiness is developed by the accruing of specific skills necessary to a substantive change in the personal mythology and thus our selfness. Our mythologies insure that we return to the scene of the trauma until we learn the missing skill(s). What ever the particular reasons for resistance, patterns of reversal occur because we are missing one or more of the essential skills required for the task. Since we will not move forwards and cannot move backwards, we slide along the horizontal or vertical axis that we cannot cross, ending up on the reverse (complementary) side of the life experiences represented by the Healing Circle. Because we are purposefully refusing to be where we are supposed to be, our act hunger to be there anyway causes us to "act out" behaviors that are metaphors of that reversed position. As we cycle through the eight gates, I attribute names and sexes to the examples. The profiles are intentionally vague, more caricatures than character studies. The skills required to cross seasonal thresholds identified below are not all-inclusive. It is important to remember that explicate diagnoses are extrapolations of data that only imperfectly apply to real live implicate humans. The personal mythology is unique and the actual profile of a person is as unrepeatable as her genome. And finally, we all share some of all categories. Our personal mythologies determine which of the gates are easy and which are difficult.